World Trade Reform

Do Developing Countries Gain or Lose?

Sheila Page
with
Michael Davenport

Overseas Development Institute

Overseas Development Institute, Regent's College, Inner Circle, Regent's Park, London NW1 4NS, UK.

A British Library Cataloguing in Publication Data record is available on request.

ISBN 0 85003 221 0

Typeset by ODI
Printed by Chameleon Press Ltd, London.

Table of Contents

Tables

Acknowledgements

In 1991, Sheila Page, Michael Davenport and Adrian Hewitt carried out a study of the effects of the probable outcome of the Uruguay Round on developing countries, published by ODI as *The GATT Uruguay Round: Effects on Developing Countries*. That arose out of discussions with officials from the Overseas Development Administration and the Foreign and Commonwealth Office, and was financed by the ODA. With the completion of the Round, the ODA and ODI decided that a new analysis was appropriate, not a simple updating of the previous report. We are very grateful to ODA for their continued interest and financial support for this work. We would like to thank the ODA officials whose comments on a preliminary version were exceptionally helpful.

We are also grateful to officials at GATT, the International Textiles and Clothing Bureau, the European Union, UNCTAD and national delegations to the international organisations who guided us through technical points and offered us invaluable insights into their implications. OECD cooperated with our repeated requests for data and use of their trade model.

Much of the discussion of the ACP countries is based on research at ODI by Antonique Koning, and the section on the Dispute Settlement procedure on a paper prepared for us by Nicolaus Luninck. Margaret Cornell's excellent editing clarified both the presentation and our analysis and Sandra Cox prepared the complex manuscripts of the joint authors for publication.

None of these is responsible for the remaining errors or our interpretation or comments. Michael Davenport had primary responsibility for Chapters 3 and 4 on agriculture and industrial tariffs, and Appendix 1 on the formerly centrally planned economies, and Sheila Page for the remaining sections.

2 December 1994

Abbreviations

ACP	African, Caribbean and Pacific (States); the developing country signatories of successive Lomé Conventions
AFTA	Asean Free Trade Area
ASEAN	Association of South-East Asian Nations
CAP	(EU) Common Agricultural Policy
CARIBCAN	Canada's Preferential Trade Scheme for the Commonwealth Caribbean
CBERA	Caribbean Basin Economic Recovery Act
CBI	Caribbean Basin Initiative (which led to the CBERA)
CMEA	Committee for Mutual Economic Assistance (same as COMECON)
EC	European Community (changed into EU from 1993); as author in references: European Commission
EFTA	European Free Trade Association
EU	European Union (formerly European Community)
FTA	free trade area
FSU	former Soviet Union
GATS	General Agreement on Trade in Services
GATT	General Agreement on Tariffs and Trade
GDP	gross domestic product
GSP	Generalised System of Preferences
ILO	International Labour Organisation
IMF	International Monetary Fund
MERCOSUR	Mercado Común del Sur (Argentina, Brazil, Paraguay, Uruguay)
MFA	Multi-Fibre Arrangement (officially the Arrangement Regarding International Trade in Textiles)
MFN	most favoured nation (the standard under GATT on WTO)
NAFTA	North American Free Trade Area
NIC	newly-industrialised country
NTB	non-tariff barrier
OAU	Organisation for African Unity
OECD	Organisation for Economic Coöperation and Development
p.e.	partial equilibrium (approach to analysis of changes in trade barriers)
PRC	Peoples' Republic of China
RUNS	Rural-urban North-South (trade model of the OECD)
SSA	Sub-Saharan Africa
STABEX	System for the Stabilisation of Export Earnings (for the ACP States under the Lomé Conventions)
SYSMIN	System for Stabilising Minerals (for the ACP States under the Lomé Conventions)
TPNG	Tropical Products Negotiating Group
UNCTAD	United Nations Conference on Trade and Development
UR	Uruguay Round of Multinational Trade Negotiations
US	United States
USDA	United States Department of Agriculture
WB	World Bank
WIPO	World Intellectual Property Organisation
WTO	World Trade Organisation (successor body to GATT)

1. Developing countries in the trade negotiations

The results of the Uruguay Round for the developing countries show three principal types of effect.

1.   Their income rises, for the conventional reasons, because of their own lower tariffs and barriers to imports and because of the potential increases in their export income derived from improved access to other countries' markets (net of any loss of production because of switches to imports).

2.   The direct gains from including temperate agricultural goods and textiles and clothing in the international trading system (although many of the reforms may come late in the 10 year implementation period) are particularly important for developing countries because these products are still significant for many of them, as exports, potential exports, or imports. The reforms also bring a major reduction in the share of their export markets which they see as operating outside normal market rules. The ending of the Multi-Fibre Arrangement is important to the net gains calculated because developing countries are net exporters and because reforms have not begun outside the Round.

3.   They regard their own decision to participate in the Round, and, following it, in the new international trading system, on level terms with the industrial countries as a necessary part of their development strategy, while they have discovered that they are seen as having useful access and other privileges for which others will negotiate.

To these must be added for both developing and industrial countries. the other, non-trade-in-goods, effects of the Round, in other economic areas, such as services and intellectual property, and more generally in the rules and functioning of the international system.

The quantifiable and unquantifiable results for old and new products and the changes in the international trading system will be discussed individually. Two changes, however, are fundamental: the extension of the system to new countries (new or newly active members) and the extension of the boundaries of what is internationally negotiable. In both of these, the Uruguay Round is equal in importance to the formation of GATT, when trade in goods was brought under international regulation. Finally, the successful completion of the Round has restored an orderly rule-based system.

Other recent Rounds have seen some extension of GATT's area of competence, for example to public procurement and some non-tariff measures in the Tokyo Round. Such an evolution is a necessary consequence of the growth in the share of trade, and of sectors, people and firms affected by trade, within national economies. Actions outside country boundaries have more impact. But the extent of the change in the Uruguay Round, including the returns of the traditional trading subjects, food and clothing, the introduction of services (and consequently migration), protection of intellectual property, and some regulation of investment, is significantly greater than in previous Rounds. The UR effectively brought all the basic factors of production (labour, technology, and capital) as well as all the normal sectors of production (services as well as goods) under one system of international regulation. It has also laid down a framework for monitoring, administering, and enforcing the system through the new powers assigned to the World Trading Organisation which will replace GATT.

For many developing countries, the Round had a further effect, parallel with the importance that the founding of GATT in 1948 had for the industrial countries. For existing members as well as for the 31 which joined during the Round, this was the negotiation in which they first participated fully, and by the end most considered GATT their principal forum for negotiations on trade. It is therefore particularly important to analyse the impact of the Round on the developing countries: more of them will be affected; all have seen more changes, by themselves and their trading partners, in sectors of interest to them than in previous Rounds. They will, therefore, be judging its impact, not simply as one Round among many, but as the first indication of the results of becoming more integrated into the international economic system. They will be passing rapidly through the stages of integration into the international economy and exposure to external economic and policy decisions through which the more developed countries have passed during the last 50 years.

The rest of this chapter will look in more detail at the reasons for this greater participation in the system, while Chapter 2 will examine the corollary, the shift, partly by their choice, partly because of demands from the advanced countries, away from 'special and different' treatment in trade, and in particular the erosion of their preferential access to industrial country markets. Chapters 3, 4 and 5 will examine and make some quantitative assessments of the effects of the Round in the three important areas for goods: agriculture, manufactures in general, and the textiles and clothing sector. These effects are summarised in Chapter 6 in order to give a quantitative indication of the impact of the Round on different types of developing country, and on a range of individual countries.

Unlike most of the available sectoral assessments for developing countries, this report will look at the potential gains in trade among developing countries, as well as in trade with the industrial countries. This is essential because some of the largest reductions in tariffs will be made (and have already been made in the course of the Round) by the developing countries in Asia and Latin America, as well as smaller cuts in some African countries. Many of the cuts are in the manufactures which the less advanced developing countries may be ready to export. Furthermore, South East Asia and China have been, and are expected to remain, the fastest growing regions, and thus to have the fastest growing demand for imports. They are becoming important markets for each other and for other developing countries. Finally, to omit the changes in policy by these countries would be to ignore the reason that developed countries specifically targeted developing countries for market access in this negotiating Round.

Any quantitative forecasts of this type are subject to uncertainties about how elastic (and how rapid) the response of demand and supply will be to the changes, and what other policies may be changed in response. These are particularly serious for developing countries where new countries and new suppliers will be entering the markets even more rapidly than in industrial countries. The inevitable assumptions that their behaviour will be the same as that of existing suppliers, and that the latter will not change as they become more experienced, are difficult to justify. In the case of tariff changes by the developing countries, the massive changes many have undertaken on their own initiatives during the course of the Round may or may not be attributable to it. Calculations for agriculture and textiles and clothing are made more difficult by the fact that these changes will be from quota- to tariff-based systems, and away from systems which have been in place throughout the entire modern development of these sectors.

Going beyond these sectoral effects: if they are large, they will in turn lead to increases in income or more dynamic effects, increasing the rate of growth of income. Trade may improve efficiency or have an accelerator effect on increasing investment. Such growth effects are conventionally seen as the most important results of the liberalisation of world trade which occurred in the 1950s and 1960s through the GATT-directed liberalisation of the world trading system (and of such regional liberalisations as the move to a Single European Market in 1993). They are difficult to measure (the problems for agriculture are discussed in Chapter 3), and standard economic forecasts and analyses have usually avoided trying to quantify them. Nevertheless, most have stressed that a settlement would bring substantial gains in world income, with a large share accruing to developing countries (and a correspondingly large loss if the Round had failed). These arguments probably contributed to developing countries' view that the gains from participating in the Round were worth some costs in terms of their own concessions. Insofar as they were derived from the traditional belief of the international agencies in the efficacy of joint action such arguments may have been inappropriate in the context of trade where major welfare gains can accrue to unilateral action, such as that already taken by the developing countries on their own barriers.

Chapters 7 to 10 will look at the results of the Uruguay Agreement which are less quantifiable. Chapter 7 (Services) will examine which types of services and under what limitations the developing countries and their trading partners have brought into the new international framework. The Round also introduces more standard forms of regulation for the other new areas, intellectual property and investment, but it will be difficult to judge the effects until there is experience in how they are applied. The final chapters will describe the new administrative structure of the WTO and its strengthened enforcement mechanisms, and ask which new subjects, and participants, are likely to be added to the agenda, as well as whether an organisation designed to regulate trade can continue to accept new types of responsibility.

The focus of this report will be on the effects on countries, not on the distribution within them. This is the necessary first step in any assessment, and corresponds to the formal and (up to now) actual structure of GATT negotiations. It is impossible to go further because of the country-by-country detail and knowledge which would be required. Some general points can, however, be suggested. The primary beneficiaries of any reduction in barriers to trade are those who purchase the imports on which tariffs or other barriers are lowered. Exporters will gain by reductions in barriers in their markets, while producers of import substitutes may lose, although their losses may be mitigated by increased demand as all incomes rise. In some cases (as will be seen particularly in the chapter on agriculture) the current distortions in the world market are so serious that removing them will cause some prices to rise, meaning that importers may lose (although increasing the gain to exporters). These are potentially serious distortions to the conclusions.

But in practice, especially in small and/or developing countries, many of these separate interests are actually the same people or companies. Clearly all are consumers. Many producers of exports and import substitutes will use imports. More generally, many people and companies may be involved in the production of a variety of products, including both import substitutes, which may lose, and exports and potential exports which will gain. It is an empirical mistake to follow the usual theoretical assumption that there will necessarily be net damage to, or opposition from, the apparent losers. Secondly, if the new system is seen as being more rule-bound and regulated than the old, there will be benefits which, it is conventionally (and probably correctly) argued, will accrue particularly to small and weak participants, and to developing countries in particular. But there may be additional gains to non-public-sector participants from the restraint which this imposes on their own governments as well as on foreign countries. Both reduce their exposure to arbitrary changes in trading conditions. The overlap within a country between losers and gainers perhaps makes a failure to examine domestic distribution less significant, while the advantages of certainty suggest that looking only at the national gains could underestimate the gains to all economic participants.

What had changed for developing countries

The share of developing countries in total trade had increased from 21% in 1973, the beginning of the previous, 'Tokyo', Round to 26% by 1986, the opening of the Uruguay Round. By 1993, it was 27%, or 28% for imports. They are now a significant part of the market for most industrial countries. Access to their markets and regulation of their trade policies were therefore objectives in the Round.

They are also competitors, even in the traditional domain of the industrial countries, exports of manufactures. Between 1970 and 1986, the beginning of the Round, their share in total world trade in manufactures rose from 7 to 12.5% (Table 1.1), reaching 20% by 1992. On their side, manufactures had increased to more than 50% of their total trade by the mid-1980s and to 73% by 1992. Agriculture and textiles and clothing, however, were still major exports (Table 1.2, about 30%), and the developing countries were increasingly unwilling to see these remain as derogations from the normal trading rules. As is clear from the tables, all these changes were most important for Asia and least important for Africa.

In the past, the scope of GATT in the areas of most interest to developing countries was limited as were exports in their own development strategies. Countries which wanted control of their own imports therefore had less reason not to limit their participation in GATT or to remain outside the system altogether. This helps to explain why major trading countries like Mexico and Venezuela did not join GATT until 1986 and 1990. The terms of this trade-off between policy freedom and rules were sharply altered in the 1970s and 1980s by their own exports and by the revival of unilateral protection through non-tariff barriers on the part of industrial countries, particularly in the goods into which the developing countries were moving, like clothing and steel. Also, the constraints, including those on agriculture and clothing, were becoming more unpredictable and more damaging, through modifications in the way in which countries applied quotas and food pricing and in the frequency with which these changed. On the other side, the increased importance of trade in developing countries' economies led to a realisation of how tightly their independence of action was limited by the non-tariff interventions of their trading partners.

The developing countries also had a new perception of what a successful trade policy was by the time this Round started. The emphasis which appeared in advice to them from the late 1970s on the importance of exports as a force for development and for industrial transformation meant that obstacles to exports were seen not just as barriers to static efficiency gains or extra costs, but as constraints on dynamic change and industrialisation. As they lowered their own barriers to imports, this perception meant that the barriers imposed

Table 1.1 Developing countries' exports of manufactures (%)

Region	1970	1980	1986	1990	1991	1992
Share of manufactures in total						
Non-oil developing countries	34	43	60	69	70	73
Asia	46	53	72	78	79	81
Latin America	22	19	31	37	36	41
Africa	7	6	14	18	18	19
Africa, non-oil exporters	9	13	19	30	26	n.a.
Shares in world exports of manufactures						
Developing countries	7.0	10.5	12.5	17.1	18.6	19.7
Asia	3.7	7.5	9.4	14.1	16.0	17.1
Latin America	1.8	1.8	1.9	2.0	1.0	2.0
Africa	0.4	0.5	0.5	0.5	0.5	0.5

Sources: IMF, *International Financial Statistics* and *Supplement on Trade Statistics;* UNCTAD, *Handbook of International Trade and Development Statistics;* UN, *Monthly Bulletin of Statistics.*

by others, and not prevented because of the imperfections in the external regulatory system,were seen as more important than the system's potential to prevent their own barriers. These considerations supplemented the perceived advantages of rules and predictability as major reasons for the increased interest of developing countries in the GATT system.

Ratification and implementation

The Uruguay Round discussions ended on 15 December 1993. The final details of the tariff and services offers were submitted and checked in the next three months, and the agreement was signed on 15 April 1994. By the end of November 1994, 36 countries had ratified it. The US voted to do so on 1 December, and Japan, the EU and Canada were expected to complete their ratifications by 21 December. The expected date for the agreement to come into force is 1 January 1995. In spite of greater than expected delays and opposition this now seems probable, and we have based our discussion on that date. Some of the issues raised in the discussions of ratification by the US and EU, however, are relevant more broadly for the future of the WTO and for other trade negotiations.

GATT has always operated on the basis that there was no equivalent of other international organisations' executive directors or security council: all negotiations are principally among the countries directly interested (the major traders in a particular commodity; the participants in a dispute). Any general discussion or (rarely) vote was then by all members. The WTO procedure will be similar, but the introduction of ministerial meetings and a stronger dispute mechanism (see Chapters 9 and 10) brought this equality into public awareness, and it was one of the issues raised in the US debates on ratification. It may be challenged in the future.

Table 1.2 Developing country exports by commodity classes and region, 1992

	Total ($m)	To Developed Countries (%)	To EU (%)	To US (%)	To Japan (%)	Share of commodities in Total [a] (%)	Share of commodities in exports to developed countries [a] (%)
All Developing Countries							
Total	927,432	57.84	20.75	21.25	11.10		
Food	91,561	60.88	26.16	15.57	15.02	9.87	10.39
Cereals	6,784	16.91	4.66	2.02	6.16	0.73	0.21
Textiles and clothing	145,028	56.19	23.32	19.14	7.82	15.64	15.19
Textile fibres	8,518	32.30	18.97	2.85	8.14	0.92	0.51
Textile, yarn & fabrics	55,725	32.17	14.57	7.63	4.69	6.01	3.34
Clothing	80,785	75.27	29.81	28.79	9.95	8.71	11.34
Chemicals	44,390	33.75	13.99	10.41	5.95	4.79	2.79
Machinery & transport	203,459	54.04	16.68	26.69	5.35	21.94	20.50
All manufactures	578,216	54.61	18.73	23.05	7.38	62.35	58.87
OPEC							
Total	179,040	65.93	26.08	19.03	17.91		
Food	6,710	60.83	26.02	18.88	13.43	3.75	3.46
Cereals	266	13.91	10.90	0.00	0.75	0.15	0.03
Textiles and clothing	9,820	46.59	26.02	11.76	4.09	5.48	3.88
Textile fibres	1,954	11.57	10.03	0.20	0.82	1.09	0.19
Textiles, yarn & fabrics	4,234	40.62	26.74	3.71	2.72	2.36	1.46
Clothing	3,632	72.38	33.78	27.37	7.46	2.03	2.23
Chemicals	5,707	31.44	17.80	4.73	4.68	3.19	1.52
Machinery & Transport	3,411	36.18	16.65	14.07	3.58	1.91	1.05
All manufactures	30,747	45.76	20.37	11.99	9.37	17.17	11.92
Non-OPEC							
Total	748,392	55.90	19.48	21.78	9.47		
Food	84,851	60.89	26.18	15.30	15.15	11.34	12.35
Cereals	6,518	17.03	4.40	2.10	6.38	0.87	0.27
Textiles and clothing	135,208	56.88	23.12	19.68	8.10	18.07	18.39
Textile fibres	6,564	38.47	21.63	3.64	10.31	0.88	0.60
Textiles, yarn & fabrics	51,491	31.48	13.57	7.96	4.85	6.88	3.87
Clothing	77,153	75.41	29.63	28.86	10.07	10.31	13.91
Chemicals	38,683	34.09	13.43	11.25	6.14	5.17	3.15
Machinery & Transport	200,048	54.34	16.68	26.90	5.38	26.73	25.99
All manufactures	547,469	55.11	18.64	23.68	7.27	73.15	72.12

Table 1.2 continued

Asia (excluding Middle East)							
Total	588,570	52.74	14.93	20.60	12.10	7.03	7.19
Food	41,357	54.00	12.88	10.06	27.60	0.69	0.21
Cereals	4,041	15.96	2.97	2.60	7.65		
Textiles and clothing	123,286	52.79	17.57	20.23	8.99	20.95	20.96
Textile fibres	5,794	24.66	11.34	2.66	9.22	0.98	0.46
Textiles, yarn & fabrics	48,689	27.85	10.71	7.08	5.19	8.27	4.37
Clothing	68,803	72.80	22.94	31.02	11.66	11.69	16.14
Chemicals	28,283	28.73	9.89	7.80	7.83	4.81	2.62
Machinery & transport	177,072	52.90	16.00	25.65	6.01	30.09	30.17
All manufactures	474,209	53.47	16.18	23.45	8.25	80.57	81.68
Latin America							
Total	135,429	66.47	21.50	36.18	5.00	24.37	25.68
Food	33,412	69.19	33.60	26.74	4.81	1.33	0.44
Cereals	1,802	21.86	7.05	1.72	6.05		
Textiles and clothing	5,442	60.82	21.15	32.52	2.26	4.02	3.68
Textile fibres	1,067	43.30	27.55	8.06	6.09	0.79	0.51
Textile, yarn & fabrics	2,482	56.20	23.37	24.29	1.85	1.83	1.55
Clothing	1,893	76.76	14.63	57.11	0.63	1.40	1.61
Chemicals	7,610	50.43	15.27	28.95	2.64	5.62	4.26
Machinery & Transport	18,302	66.03	12.02	47.96	1.37	13.51	13.43
All manufactures	55,455	60.36	16.41	35.99	4.20	40.95	37.19
Africa							
Total	70,120	82.43	58.19	18.15	2.29	12.67	11.48
Food	8,885	74.71	56.43	5.41	6.52	0.32	0.06
Cereals	224	14.29	8.48	0.00	0.00		
Textiles and clothing	5,423	82.78	71.38	5.88	1.70	7.73	7.77
Textile fibres	1,159	55.05	39.60	0.09	7.51	1.65	1.10
Textile yarn & fabrics	1,020	68.82	54.90	6.27	0.49	1.45	1.21
Clothing	3,244	97.07	87.92	7.83	0.00	4.63	5.45
Chemicals	2,507	44.83	42.68	0.60	0.20	3.58	1.94
Machinery & Transport	1,192	56.46	50.67	1.68	0.00	1.70	1.16
All manufactures	13,084	71.98	58.87	5.32	4.51	18.66	16.29

(a) Percentages do not add to 100 because of omitted categories

Source: UN, *Monthly Bulletin of Statistics,* May 1994.

8

There was particular opposition to the more automatic and enforceable nature of the dispute settlement procedure (see Chapter 9). This led to commitments to continue to use existing US legislation providing for bilateral pressure and action in spite of GATT/WTO rules. The US carried forward disputes with both Japan and Canada after April, completely outside GATT procedures. The ratification included provision for judicial review of WTO rulings. The EU has also considered restricting the applicability of WTO decisions. These reservations could reduce the confidence and certainty effects of the settlement and of all international agreements, but experience will show whether they prove more damaging than the implicit reservations of the (perceived) national interest behind any international agreement.

The issues of social standards and the environment (see Chapter 10) raised by the US at the final signing in April 1994 were also raised in the Congressional discussion. It is increasingly clear that these will be brought into future trade negotiations, in and outside the WTO.

By US budgetary law, any proposal which may reduce tax revenues must incorporate an offsetting change. (Economists' forecasts of medium-term balancing effects as incomes rise are not a valid substitute.) Ratifying the negotiated cuts in tariffs therefore required either an alternative tax or an explicit waiver to accompany the ratification. This offered an additional focus for opposition and opportunity for delay, and one which could apply to any trade agreement, including concessions of preferences or regional pacts. For the UR, a waiver was eventually accepted.

The US negotiated and ratified the UR agreement (and NAFTA) under the authority of 'fast track' provisions, which ensured that any agreement could only be accepted or rejected, not amended. The administration failed to obtain an extension of this beyond the end of 1994 which means that it will have to obtain an explicit equivalent authority whenever it enters another trade negotiation. This was the normal position in the past (it was the extended period of the UR negotiations and the corresponding extension of the 'fast track' granted for them that was unusual), but it could make further regional negotiations with Latin America, for example, more difficult.

The EU faced two difficulties on ratification procedure. The first was mainly technical, on the correct procedure under the new post-Maastricht provisions, in particular the role of the European Parliament in international agreements. 1994 was, however, a sensitive time in relations between the Commission and the Parliament for such questions to arise, and the fact that it was raised for such a conspicuous issue as GATT ratification meant that there has been caution about bringing forward other agreements (including the new Community scheme for GSP (the Generalised System of Preferences for developing countries).

The Commission submitted the agreement to Parliament in November 1994. This requirement will make approval of future agreements negotiated by the Commission and Council of Ministers, whether international or bilateral, less automatic than in the past.

The other more serious difficulty was whether the EU, rather than the members, had the legal competence to make international agreements on those issues which have not been assigned to it by its members. It was given negotiating authority, but it was explicitly stated that this did not give it competence to make the agreements. The questions raised were about trade in services, services which come under the new agreement, but which are not actually traded (they are provided to or by foreign nationals within the host country), and intellectual property. Some of the first have been transferred to the EU as being closely tied to trade in goods; the second and third have not been. The question was raised at the time the agreement was signed in April, and to avoid doubts the EU and all the members signed. It was then referred to the European Court of Justice which ruled that the EU did have competence for traded services, as part of its competence in commercial policy, but that the member states retained competence in the other matters. This was, however, shared competence, not exclusive to the members because such services are related to trade and subject to harmonisation obligations. For the specific case of the UR negotiations, this meant that both the members and the EU had to ratify.

For the future, particularly if the WTO evolves into an organisation in which negotiations about modifications to the agreements take place continuously, not in Rounds and if new subjects are brought into it as they become important or recognised as of international concern (see Chapter 10), the lack of exclusive competence for either the EU or its members will be an obstacle. Various member countries have particular interests in some services, particularly in finance or shipping. If the EU is able to extend its authority to negotiate, if not to ratify, this, like the US fast track authority, could reduce, but not remove the difficulty and delay of requiring that each country and the European Parliament approve any agreements.

For both the US and EU, the question of shared authority, with Congress and the states or with the member countries, has always been a problem in trade negotiations. The difficulties over ratification in 1994 and those created by the extension of trade negotiations into related areas will intensify this.

2. Preferences and other differential treatment

From 1971, GATT allowed developing countries to receive non-reciprocal (and non-MFN) preferential access to developed country markets and also to have greater freedom in controlling their own imports, for development or balance of payments reasons. As they could also avoid 'binding' their tariffs (i.e. notifying their structure to GATT and agreeing to make no upward adjustments), this gave them and their trading partners two means to use trade policy to assist development. This system of special treatment was transformed in the 1980s, and was further eroded by their participation in the Uruguay Round. As discussed in Chapter 1, many developing countries no longer want to protect their imports. The questions which have faced developing countries throughout the Uruguay Round, and which will continue to do so as they adjust to the new regime, are whether the preferences and privileges which they have lost in the Round were sufficiently compensated by their gains in other aspects of tariff access or on other issues, and whether their remaining concessions are sufficiently valuable to be worth their pressing hard to retain them and to restore their value.

Restricting the right to control imports

The UR agreement restricts developing countries' greater freedom to use direct controls under the balance-of-payments provisions; they are now expected to use tariffs (Agosin *et al.*, 1994) (although experience in developed countries suggests that 'crises' frequently lead to nominally non-allowable measures). But in practice, both GATT and other international organisations have put increasing pressure on the most advanced, especially the NICs, not to use their right to impose import controls for balance-of-payments reasons, and several developing countries have now renounced it. More important for long-term strategy, under the Uruguay Round settlement, developing countries have now bound their tariffs, effectively ending their freedom to change back to the protectionist instruments of the past. Unlike most of the other effects to be analysed here, this takes effect as soon as the Agreement comes into force and its legal force derives entirely from the Agreement, not from unilateral actions.

All the Latin American and most of the Asian countries have not only lowered their tariffs, but bound them. The proportion bound by all developing countries has risen from 13% to 61% (measured by share of imports covered). Within this, Latin America has risen from 57% to 100% and Asia from 32% to 70% (GATT 1994 *Access*,[1] with amendments). 71% of the Latin American imports which are bound and 38% of the Asian are at a lower level than before the Round. The general level for Latin America is about 35%; most countries have chosen to specify a general rather than product-by-product binding. Although for many developing countries these bound levels are in fact above the currently applied rate (Mexico, for example, reduced its bound tariff from 50% to 35%, while its applied tariffs have fallen from 23% to 13% since the beginning of the Round) (GATT 1993 *Mexico*), the binding is still an important limit on their future policy. The South East Asian countries have given much more specific undertakings. Africa in general has not increased bindings, or only at very high ceilings. For agricultural goods, the changes are more striking, an increase from 25% to 100% for all developing countries. For Latin America and Asia the previous levels were 74% and 40%. 85% of the Latin American bindings and 74% of the Asian represent reductions in tariffs.

---

1. References to different publications by the same organisation will be distinguished by adding a key word from the title.

One compensating gain is the increased level of binding in their markets, especially in agriculture by the developed countries. The developed countries had already bound most of their tariffs on industrial products (the UR increased the level only from 94% to 99%), but the tariffication of previous agricultural controls (discussed in Chapter 3) raised bindings here from 81% to 100%. The increase in binding by all countries means greatly increased security of access (although the developing countries gain less than the industrial, except in their developing country markets). There is also an important technical gain from the switch to tariffs in agriculture: in contrast to the position on manufactures, the possibilities of offering preferences to developing countries is increased. It is now possible to extend preferences in the form of lower tariffs to these products. In the past some countries have had special privileges in the form of quotas on particular agricultural products, but it was not possible to bring these into a standard scheme.

Lowering the scope for preferences

On the other side, the lowering of standard MFN, Most Favoured Nation, tariff rates (the official level negotiated under GATT) has reduced the possible scope and significance of preferences (especially for manufactures). Industrial countries had already substantially lowered their tariffs in previous rounds; Table 2.1 indicates how limited the post-Tokyo Round margins between MFN and GSP rates were in most products, but the Uruguay Round negotiations further reduced the potential for offering a preference. In many cases the MFN rate is now below the GSP rate, and on some products it has fallen to zero.[2] Although the GSP rates are being revised, so far no developed country has adjusted its GSP scheme to restore margins, and for the many developing country manufactures for which GSP already gives no tariff or which are now zero tariff within the MFN, it is clearly impossible to restore the margin of preference. In any case, the advantages of a differential, given low remaining tariffs, in most cases will be negligible.

The effects of a preference are (like those of a customs union) trade *creation* (allowing imports from the developing country to compete more effectively with those produced in the home country) and trade *diversion* (giving developing country exports an advantage over other exporters). Reducing the preference by lowering the barriers to others reduces the diversion and allows some of the creation effects to be transferred to other suppliers. This is often called diversion, but it needs to be distinguished from traditional diversion. It will normally improve efficient allocation of production. It is, however, not a simple 'undiversion' because it is combined with an increase in creation so that the trade flows and patterns which emerge are new. We will call it *trade shift*.

Although the immediate effect of reductions in some MFN rates is to cut preferences, MFN tariffs are far from being irrelevant to developing countries. For a number of reasons, many of their exports do not receive GSP treatment. This includes exports to other developing countries as well as the product exceptions already mentioned. (The transition economies in Eastern Europe, Russia, and the Ukraine do offer GSP schemes.) Because GSP schemes are not contractual and donors can withdraw the privileges on individual products or countries

---

2. Pharmaceuticals, construction equipment, medical equipment, steel, beer, furniture, farm equipment, spirits, wood, paper and toys.

12

Table 2.1: Post-Tokyo Round MFN and GSP tariffs in selected industrial countries

Product Group	MFN Tariffs				Average Applied				GSP Tariffs			
	EC	Japan	US	All Developed	EC	Japan	US	All Developed	EC	Japan	US	All Developed
All food items	3.7	9.7	4.1	6.4	4.4	9.4	3.5	5.3	5.0	11.1	3.6	5.5
Food and live animals	3.2	10.0	3.8	6.5	4.8	9.7	3.2	5.3	5.1	11.7	3.4	5.6
Oilseeds and nuts	10.3	5.6	1.4	5.3	4.9	4.8	1.0	4.0	6.2	5.0	0.3	4.5
Animal and vegetable oils	0.1	0.3	0.9	0.1	0.0	0.3	1.0	0.2	0.0	1.2	0.1	0.4
Agricultural raw materials	3.4	0.7	0.3	0.8	0.4	0.3	0.3	0.5	0.5	0.5	0.1	0.5
Ores and metals	2.8	2.5	1.9	2.3	0.7	1.8	2.2	1.5	0.5	1.3	1.1	0.9
Iron and steel	5.5	5.0	4.3	5.1	2.3	2.9	5.0	3.4	3.3	2.0	3.5	3.0
Nonferrous metals	3.2	5.5	0.7	2.3	0.5	4.3	0.7	1.3	0.5	3.1	0.3	1.1
Fuels	0.1	1.5	0.4	1.1	0.3	1.2	0.4	0.6	0.2	1.3	0.3	0.6
Chemicals	8.4	5.5	3.7	5.8	3.4	4.8	3.9	3.1	4.1	5.1	1.0	3.7
Manufactures excl. chemicals	8.1	5.7	5.6	7.0	4.6	4.6	4.9	4.7	6.4	4.2	6.6	6.7
Leather	10.2	11.9	4.2	5.1	2.1	10.7	2.7	3.1	2.8	8.4	1.4	3.2
Textile yarn and fabrics	17.3	8.6	10.6	11.7	5.3	7.1	12.1	7.9	7.6	6.1	9.0	8.4
Clothing	19.9	15.0	20.3	17.5	7.3	10.0	18.1	11.9	9.3	8.6	17.8	14.6
Footwear	22.5	14.2	11.7	13.4	6.5	12.5	9.5	9.0	9.1	7.9	9.4	10.1
Other items	4.8	2.3	n.a.	n.a.	0.1	0.7	3.6	3.3	0.1	1.0	0.4	3.8
All products	4.2	3.5	3.9	4.7	2.5	3.1	3.8	3.0	2.1	2.3	3.6	2.7
Developing country weights	3.2	3.0	4.9	n.a.	2.1	2.4	4.5	n.a.	2.1	2.3	3.6	2.7

Source: Finger and Olechowski (1987).

Table 2.2: Erosion of GSP margins (%)

	European Union					Japan				USA			
	Preferential Margin		Margin Loss	Africa ACP lost margin (6)	Africa GSP Lost Margin (6)	Preferential Margin		Margin Loss	Africa GSP Lost Margin (6)	Preferential Margin		Margin Loss	Africa GSP Lost Margin (6)
	PRE UR	POST UR				PRE UR	POST UR			PRE UR	POST UR		
All GSP items	8.42	5.70	2.72	3.91	3.35	6.73	2.61	4.12	3.23	4.87	2.44	2.43	1.66
Agriculture non tropical	6.02	1.89	4.13	13.01	5.20	15.77	5.59	10.18	5.83	7.41	5.04	2.37	0.52
Agriculture tropical	4.27	1.11	3.16	4.72	2.93	21.18	7.23	13.95	3.86	7.17	4.71	2.46	3.79
Tropical non-agricultural	6.92	3.56	3.36	3.34	3.35	6.53	1.77	4.76	4.89	3.97	1.17	2.80	1.80
Natural Resource Based Products	8.30	5.38	2.92	2.00	3.55	4.25	1.58	2.67	3.21	4.25	3.19	1.06	1.27
Textiles (a)	11.94	10.15	1.79	1.79	1.79	7.98	3.59	4.39	4.31	4.84	3.21	1.63	3.59
Manufactured leather and footwear	10.36	8.86	1.50	2.06	3.19	9.07	7.38	1.69	0.00	4.33	2.11	2.02	0.77
Other industrial products	7.44	4.30	3.14	1.83	2.70	5.70	1.97	3.73	3.09	4.85	2.27	2.58	2.56

Notes: No account has been taken of special rates applicable to LDCs in Japan

Averages: Weighted averages are calculated from lines for which preferential rates (ACP and GSP) exist and total import value for the tariff line is not less than $1000.

Loss of Preference is calculated as the difference between the old and new preferential margins at the end of the adjustment period.

(a) As textiles were not included in the US GSP regime and only for minor exporters in the EU GSP, these results are puzzling.

Source: UNCTAD, 1994 *GSP*; OAU, 1994

at their own discretion, whether for the policy reasons discussed above or for individual reasons, the effective binding is the rate at which the MFN tariff is bound.

UNCTAD (1994 *GSP*) has made preliminary estimates of the erosion of GSP margins (apparently with no allowance for other preference schemes) (Table 2.2). This shows relatively small changes overall (2% for the US, 3% for the EU and 4% for Japan), but relatively large changes for agriculture, both tropical and temperate. The latter does not include the changes from quotas to tariffs. The products on which GSP is important now are industrial products other than clothing, and here the change is close to the average. The losses for the poorest area, Africa, appear similar in the US and Japanese markets, but they are larger precisely in the agricultural sectors which are important to them. The losses are also large relative to the preference margins which they have in the EU from ACP membership. This could be interpreted to suggest that the actual structure of MFN tariff cuts is going in the opposite direction from the intention to provide more preference to the low income countries, but it means that the cuts in legally binding protection have been greatest in these products.

Product coverage of GSP will be reduced by the new zero MFN tariffs, by about 15–20%. This reduction of some tariffs to zero emerged from the use in the Uruguay Round of a product-by-product approach to tariff cutting (instead of a percentage-based formula as in the Tokyo Round). Another result of this form of negotiation was that the MFN tariffs on sensitive products, frequently those on which GSP is not applied, were cut least.

The EU has prepared a new scheme (EC, 1994 *GSP*). It will avoid the problem of adjusting the remaining GSP tariffs to keep up with MFN reductions by expressing the preference as a percentage reduction of the MFN rate (tariff modulation), rather than as a fixed lower rate as in the past. The 'modulations' are 20% for 'sensitive' goods or 40% for 'semi-sensitive', with zero tariffs for the rest. The declared intention is to maintain the same proportional reduction as before the Uruguay Round settlement although it is not clear how this is possible in the cases of GSP or MFN zero tariffs. Maintaining the margin in percentage terms is an erosion of the absolute level of preference. Its implementation can also be restricted in the case of some 'sensitive' products. In other countries' GSPs (for example Australia, UNCTAD, 1994 *GSP*), goods for which the MFN rate is at or below the GSP rate have simply been removed from the GSP scheme. The former EFTA countries will adopt the EU GSP scheme as it is at the time of their entry: this will probably mean a small reduction in access.

The restrictions on the GSP scheme

Although, as discussed in Chapter 4, there are still high tariffs on some goods of interest to developing country exporters, these are frequently those excluded from GSP schemes. The EU scheme excludes many minerals and metals, starches, and some categories of leather. It excludes clothing, except for countries which are restricted under the MFA. It frequently limits the quantities admitted on GSP terms. Japan excludes all processed foods, and also controls textiles and clothing. All schemes have safeguard clauses, although other devices for excluding particular products from particular countries have been used more frequently. The EU uses tariff quotas on sensitive imports.

In the US GSP 'competitive needs criteria' provide for the withdrawal of the preference when exports from one country of a particular product reach a certain level. All schemes have strictly applied rules of origin, which reduce their usefulness to developing country exporters. Moreover, the exporters sometimes find the schemes uneconomic. Where the preference margin is small, the transactions costs or production costs imposed by rules of origin may outweigh the benefits.

The significance of these problems with the scheme is suggested by the fact that, for the OECD as a whole, only about half of imports covered actually received preferences (UNCTAD, 1994 *GSP*), with the rate for the EU slightly below the average (although it had risen from 44 % to 48 % between 1990 and 1992). About three quarters of the EU's imports were covered by the scheme. There was a 2 point reduction in utilisation of the Japanese GSP (to 46%); this was attributed to reductions in its MFN duties. The US figure is 46%. For the least developed countries, almost all dutiable imports are covered by the EU scheme, again with a utilisation rate of about 50%. For Japan, the utilisation rate is higher for covered goods, at 62%, but this is because only three quarters of developing country exports to Japan are covered by GSP; the share of GSP in total dutiable imports into Japan is lower than in the other importers, at 45%.

This means that the share of total imports from GSP beneficiaries which actually receive GSP treatment is often very low. For the OECD as a whole, the share in 1992 was 23.7%, for the US 14.5%, for Japan 16%, and for the EU 32.9%. For the US in 1991 the shares were 11.0% for agricultural goods and 14.8% for industrial goods and for the EU the shares were 20.2 and 17.9% respectively (Davenport, 1994).

Who benefits from preferences?

In many of its provisions, including the extent to which general and agricultural subsidies are now permitted and the rules on intellectual property, the UR settlement makes a three way distinction among developed countries, middle-income countries (called 'developing'), and the least developed. The second group are given more time (typically 50%), or allowed to make a smaller reduction (typically two thirds) in implementing each article. The third group are effectively exempted from many requirements. The second group are not defined within the agreement, and up to now there has been no formal method of defining them or determining when a country should graduate from the classification. This informal system could survive because the privileges granted under the old GATT rules were mainly permissive: the countries could have different trade provisions of their own, or other countries could offer them privileges bilaterally. In principle other countries could challenge the classification (by making a complaint that an exemption or a privilege was contrary to GATT rules because the beneficiary was not a developing country), but until recently this was not done. The EU has now lodged objections to Korea, Hong Kong and Singapore. The US has excluded them in its legislation implementing the WTO. There is no GATT or WTO procedure to deal with either attempt to exclude them. But there are now formal WTO obligations varying with the classification. The GATT system under which countries, could declare themselves to be developing (or to be graduated as Spain and Portugal did when they joined the EC) becomes legally untenable. The bilateral concessionary schemes have operated arbitrarily, with each industrial country choosing its own definition. The definition of 'least developed' will be the UN definition, but as this excludes some low-income countries and was not designed to measure trade competitiveness, it may also need rethinking.

There is a tendency now in both the UR settlement and in the operation of GSP and other preference schemes to concentrate the advantages on the least developed countries. 'Graduation' of the higher-income countries from GSP status will continue. The US has already graduated four Gulf states and four Asian NICs, and will graduate Israel in 1995. It has proposed lowering the income limit at which it has discretion to graduate a country in its new (post-1994) scheme (from $11,389 to $7,000, clearly moving towards eliminating the NICs). It could then designate almost all exports by least developed countries as eligible for GSP. The new EU proposals on GSP explicitly target the least developed (EC, 1994 *Role of GSP*). They envisage removing not only the most advanced countries, but the more advanced middle income countries, probably on a staged and product by product basis, with the intention of ultimately concentrating preferences on the lowest income countries (EC 94 GSP). At present the middle income countries and the NICs are the principal users of all the major countries' GSP schemes (Table 2.3), so that these reforms will lower significantly the share of imports entering on GSP terms.

Because many of the least developed are members of the ACP group which receives more generous terms than the GSP, their potential gains from GSP privileges, even if these are enhanced, are small (Table 2.4). At present, the least developed countries account for 1% of imports from GSP beneficiaries and 2% of GSP utilisation (EC, 1994 *Role of GSP*). The exceptions among the low-income countries are India and China which have consistently been among the major users of GSP schemes, with China now leading in both the EU and the Japanese schemes (Table 2.3). These are not, however, in formal definition, least developed, and China could have its present access to the EU scheme limited, under the proposed 'solidarity' mechanism which would restrict countries whose exports 'covered by the GSP in a given sector exceeded a certain percentage (15–25%) of all beneficiaries' exports of those products in that sector' (EC, 1994, *Role of GSP*). The rationale behind this, and other references to some countries crowding out access of the least developed seems to be that there is a limited market in the EU for some goods, with competition only among imports, not between imports and domestic production.

The potential impact on middle-income countries, however, may be large because GSP at present covers a high proportion of their exports. For Thailand, for example, more than 80% of its manufactures exports to each of the EU, US, and Japan are eligible for GSP, and the proportion has risen sharply since 1986 (from around 70%) because of the shift into electrical and electronic goods (and away from clothing) (Chirathivat, 1991, 1992–93). These figures may, however, overestimate GSP's importance to Thailand because they make no allowance for under-utilisation (and because of the small absolute importance of many preferences).

There has been further erosion of the preference system within GATT because new (or returning) developing country members have not been allowed as extensive an exemption from tariff binding or from the rules on non-tariff barriers as existing members. Mexico had to make strong commitments. The accession of China is being negotiated effectively on a developed country basis although by any income or structural standard it is a developing country member. South Africa has been given an intermediate, transitional status.

Table 2.3: Imports of major preference-giving countries from their major users of preferences 1992 (US $m.)

	Covered imports as % dutiable	Use of preferences as % covered	Share in country's GSP imports
OECD			
EU	47.8	49.5	
China	86.7	49.3	24.0
India	94.6	62.6	8.2
Thailand	69.8	54.2	7.2
Brazil	59.6	63.4	7.0
Indonesia	86.2	56.6	6.9
Singapore	92.2	34.8	6.2
Malaysia	94.7	43.9	5.8
Rep of Korea	86.3	25.3	5.7
Hong Kong	43.3	23.5	2.0
Pakistan	93.4	59.0	2.9
Philippines	90.1	47.7	2.2
Mexico	87.0	52.5	2.3
Sub-total	80.6	46.2	80.4
Total	68.5	48.0	100
Japan			
China	63.3	20.8	14.8
Rep. of Korea	69.8	50.4	22.6
Taiwan (Province of China)	57.3	67.3	17.3
Brazil	72.9	91.1	6.5
Malaysia	44.2	80.0	5.0
Thailand	43.1	44.9	4.8
Indonesia	15.2	49.8	4.0
Sub total	53.7	43.2	75.1
Total	34.7	46.1	100
US (1991)			
Mexico	49.7	29.1	28.1
Malaysia	71.3	71.5	14.1
Thailand	54.1	63.2	10.8
Brazil	41.9	64.3	9.5
Philippines	42.3	80.8	6.0
Indonesia	25.8	52.3	2.6
Sub-total	49.3	44.3	71.1
Total	36.3	50.8	100

Source: UNCTAD, 1994 *GSP*.

Table 2.4: Weighted tariff averages [a] on Sub-Saharan African countries' exports to the EC, Japan and the US

Exporter	EC		Japan		United States	
	Facing the exporter	*Facing all developing*	*Facing the exporter*	*Facing all Developing*	*Facing the Exporter*	*Facing all Developing*
Total	0.01	1.75	1.64	1.71	0.48	6.63
Angola	0.0	0.7	0.0	0.0	0.7	0.8
Benin*	0.0	0.5	4.1	0.5	0.7	4.0
Botswana	0.0	1.7	0.8	0.1	1.8	15.3
Burkina Faso*	0.0	1.3	0.6	1.3	8.6	11.1
Burundi*	0.0	1.9	0.0	0.0	0.2	1.7
Cameroon	0.0	0.9	1.1	3.2	0.8	3.5
Cape Verde	0.0	2.1	..	..	0.0	0.0
C.A.R.*	0.0	1.6	0.0	0.0	0.4	5.0
Chad*	0.0	1.6	0.0	0.0	29.9	32.0
Comoros*	0.0	2.2	0.2	0.1	0.7	7.5
Congo	0.0	0.6	0.0	0.0	0.6	0.7
Djibouti*	0.0	1.9	1.9	5.0	2.2	6.0
Eq. Guinea	0.0	1.5			17.0	27.7
Ethiopia*	0.0	1.7	0.2	0.1	0.3	3.5
Gabon	0.0	0.9	0.0	0.0	0.7	3.5
Gambia*	0.0	1.9	0.5	4.0	0.0	1.2
Ghana	0.0	1.4	0.4	1.2	0.0	1.8
Guinea*	0.0	1.6	0.8	4.3	0.0	4.0
Guinea-B*	0.0	1.1	0.5	4.0	0.7	4.3
Ivory Coast	0.0	1.2	0.2	0.1	0.1	4.1
Kenya	0.0	1.7	3.1	1.7	0.6	7.1
Lesotho*	0.0	1.8	0.0	5.6	13.6	18.6
Liberia	0.0	1.2	0.0	0.0	0.0	6.1
Madagascar	0.0	1.4	1.6	1.9	0.0	2.4
Malawi*	0.0	1.7	0.0	0.0	11.1	3.7
Mali*	0.0	1.3	4.3	3.4	1.9	7.9
Mauritania*	0.0	1.3	0.7	4.1	4.3	11.5
Mauritius	0.0	2.1	2.6	5.1	14.4	8.7
Mozambique*	0.0	1.0	2.9	2.6	0.2	2.5
Namibia	..	..	..	..	0.4	1.4
Niger*	0.0	0.6	0.0	0.0	0.9	4.4
Nigeria	0.0	0.8	2.6	3.1	0.7	2.0
Reunion	..	..	..	..	..	..
Rwanda*	0.0	1.8	0.0	0.0	0.3	5.9
Sao Tome*	0.0	2.3	..	..	1.9	3.5
Senegal	0.0	1.4	3.4	2.3	2.6	9.2
Seychelles	0.0	2.1	3.5	4.6	3.3	6.7
Sierra Leone*	0.0	1.2	3.0	3.0	0.7	5.8
Somalia*	0.0	2.2	0.0	0.0	6.1	8.7
Sudan*	0.0	1.2	0.0	0.1	1.1	18.5
Swaziland	0.0	2.4	0.0	0.0	2.2	7.9
Tanzania	0.0	1.6	0.2	1.3	0.4	1.0
Togo*	0.0	1.3	0.0	0.0	0.0	3.8
Uganda*	0.0	1.6	0.0	0.0	0.0	1.6
Zaire	0.0	0.8	0.0	0.1	0.5	1.0
Zambia	0.0	2.1	0.0.	0.1	0.7	2.0
Zimbabwe	0.0	2.0	1.2	0.1	3.2	8.1

Source: Erzan and Svedberg, 1989.

[a] Trade weighted actual average tariffs in 1986, including preferences. The average for the individual SSA country is based on its own trade weights in the market concerned. The corresponding average for 'all developing' is restricted to the same products; however it uses aggregate trade weights of all developing countries. All are members of the ACP.

* Least developed countries according to the UN.

Reliability of preferences

The predictability and value of GSP schemes have been reduced because they can be extended or withdrawn for non-developmental reasons. In 1990, Colombia, Peru, Bolivia, and Ecuador were are given enhanced GSP privileges by both the US and the EU in order to promote non-cocaine exports. These created uncertainty about future preferences, and relative preferences, in the Andean countries and their competitors. The EC scheme was initially only for four years, and thus was considered too uncertain to use effectively by the exporters in recipient countries. It was extended, but Venezuela has been added and the EU has proposed removing preferences from some products. The EC extended GSP to the Eastern European countries (before they were granted even greater preferences), and the US also added them to its GSP (as well as some of the developing countries from the former Soviet Union area). Both the US and the EU extended their schemes to South Africa in 1994. The US has proposed ending its exclusion of OPEC members (in force since 1974).

Both the US and the EU offer greater preferences for selected closely associated countries, notably the Caribbean (the Caribbean Basin Initiative countries), for the US (and its reciprocal agreement with Mexico) and the ACP countries under the Lomé Convention for the EU (and more recently the eastern European). Having more than one scheme means that members of each are indirectly vulnerable to improvements in the others, without any effective right (the Lomé countries have a formal right) to consultation or compensation. (In contrast, under GATT and WTO provisions, except in the specific cases of general special treatment for all developing countries or free trade areas, alterations in bilateral arrangements which affect third countries are subject to provisions for consultation and compensation.)

The US has used withdrawal (and more often threats of withdrawal) of GSP preferences to encourage countries to raise labour standards (on a discretionary, not uniform basis across all developing countries, and with performance assessed unilaterally by the US). Syria and Mauritania were removed from the US GSP during 1993, joining 8 other ex-members, and 13 others were under review (UNCTAD, 1994 *GSP*) (and therefore under uncertainty) during that year. The new EU scheme creates greater than normal reductions in MFN tariffs to encourage environmental or social reforms (again on the basis of unilateral EU judgement). The application of labour standard criteria could be used against both the major low-income GSP users, India and China, effectively leaving no gainers from GSP. In the past the US has also used GSP to encourage countries to protect patents and copyright (Thailand was partially excluded in 1992 for that reason); it is not clear whether this will continue now that these are under GATT regulation (perhaps an example of erosion of lack of preference). The EU has suggested introducing intellectual property, but has made no formal proposal.

Against these losses of exemption from some controls and of special access for some exports must be set the gains on general tariff cuts and bindings, the gains in particular areas like agriculture and clothing and textiles (discussed in subsequent chapters), and the possible gains from greater negotiating strength because developing countries are now participating more often on the same terms as developed countries.

20

Preferences as micro, rather than macro instruments

Past studies have suggested that the importance of GSP cannot be measured by broad measures, of margin of preference or coverage, but derives from its promotional character. Trade preferences, like import protection have traditionally been seen as giving an initial boost to industrialisation or, at least, to the further processing of primary products to replace exports of basic foodstuffs, minerals and other resource-based products whose world income elasticity appears low. They are seen as a spur to investment in new export sectors and a generator of employment opportunities. Now the preference margin will be totally eliminated in some sectors, including large parts of the machinery and electro-technical industries, metal industries, wood processing and paper, pharmaceutical and certain other chemical industries. Developing countries entering new export markets will face sharper competition, not only that from other developing countries excluded from GSP schemes or those whose preferences were quota-constrained because they had already established their competitiveness, but from the industrial countries.

The GSP scheme has not, however, been well-adapted to providing this type of stimulus. The administrative complications limited its use, as already mentioned. In many countries there is evidence that it has been more used by experienced exporters (perhaps when introducing a new product, or, in the case of foreign investors, a new supplying country) than by inexperienced exporters. The limits on imported inputs imposed by the rules of origin have also reduced its usefulness at early stages of production and export, as domestic suppliers may only emerge once a product has itself acquired a sufficiently large and secure market to justify them.

Though the preference may serve as a catalyst for developing a dynamic export sector, it may not be either a necessary or a sufficient condition. Other factors – the depth of the infrastructure, the availability of entrepreneurial skills, the sufficiency of investment funds, the adequacy of incentives, the climate for foreign investment, the appropriateness of the policy framework, among many others – could each be more important. If the beneficiary countries are seriously lacking in one or more of these, it could be that, even where their margins of preference are highest, they are inadequate to compensate for the deficiency.

In general, the point at which countries have benefited appears to have been when they were moving into more advanced industrial exports (the less advanced, especially clothing, are resricted or excluded). For Thailand, for example, this was the 1980s; for Mauritius, the benefits from its ACP membership (including on clothing) also came in the late 1980s. Under the proposed shift downwards of GSP to the least developed, privileges might start to be withdrawn precisely at this point.

The instrument offered by the Uruguay Round settlement for developing country difficulties is technical assistance (Table 2.5). As indicated in the survey of African countries quoted earlier, this is seen as a need by developing countries, but it will not fully meet the specific gap of assistance in entering markets. It is concentrated on meeting the new costs from increased regulations, rather than the traditional cost of bringing a new product to competitiveness.

Table 2.5 Uruguay Round references to technical assistance

Subject	Type of assistance	Agent
Balance of payments	Preparing documentaion for consultations	WTO
Customs valuation	Training personnel, preparing implementation measures, studies of problems of concern to developing countries	Customs Cooperation Council
Dispute settlement	A legal expert for legal advice and assistance	WTO Technical Coopration Services
Food imports	Promotion of agricultural productivity and infrastructure	Bilateral aid programs
Least developed countries	On expansion and diversification of production and exports	Unspecified
Notification procedures	Meeting notification obligations	Council for Trade in Goods and others
Preshipment inspection	General	Bi-, pluri- or multilateral basis
Services	General	WTO
Sanitary measures	processing technologies, research, infrastructure, training; investment required for fulfilling sanitary requirements of an importing country; notification	Bilateral or multilateral; WTO
Technical barriers	Preparation of regulations; creation of standardizing bodies and legal framework for meeting obligations of regional or international agreements on conformity assessment; information for procedures on conformity assessment procedures; special efforts for least developed countries	Developed countries
Telecommunications	Information for strengthening domestic telecommunications sector; cooperation amongst developing countries; for least-developed countries, foreign suppliers to assist in technology transfer and training	Governments and public telecommunications suppliers to develop programs of ITU, UNDP, IBRD
TRIPs	For least-developed countries incentives for promotion of technology transfer; for all developing countries preparation of legislation on protection and enforcement of intellectual property; personnel training	Developed country enterprises and institutions
TPRM	Compilation of information on trade policies	WTO

Source: Weston (1994)

Other preferences : ACP, CBI

For countries which are members of more preferential schemes, notably the ACP countries for the EU and Mexico and the Caribbean for the US, the losses from erosion of preferences amd trade shift may be greater. They have more to lose in terms of margin, and they have less to gain because they were less restricted in other ways, by quotas or by uncertainty. The major opening negotiated between the US and Mexico (especially on the side of Mexico) was in agriculture; the GATT reform of agricultural trade could therefore substantially reduce the NAFTA advantages for both (and also reduce the potential diversion of trade from other developing countries). Manufactured goods already had access to the US, under either special processing schemes or the GSP, so Mexico can only lose from general tariff cuts on these, but the levels of tariff were so low that the changes in margin are unlikely to have large effects.

Under Lomé IV, ACP exporters have tariff- and quota-free entry into the EU market with respect to all manufactured goods except rum, which is subject to a duty-free quota. ACP states are not subject to MFA quotas. For agricultural goods there are special preferences, generally tariff-free and NTB-free access for products not produced under Common Agricultural Policy regimes or not competitive with such products (e.g. cane sugar). For CAP or CAP-competitive goods, including rice, there is generally some reduction in the tariff or a variable levy.

One particular product, bananas, can be taken care of at this point. A new and controversial regime was established by the EU and came into operation in 1994. Up to 1993 the EU market was compartmentalised with certain Member States maintaining quotas or import prohibitions to preserve markets for their 'traditional' suppliers. These mechanisms were inconsistent with the 1992 Single European Market. The difficulty in finding a mechanism which continued to give special access to the traditional suppliers in the Caribbean and Africa within a single market for bananas was compounded by the need to invent a regime that could be justified under GATT rules, particularly in a year when the UR negotiations were coming to a head. Efforts to make the regime 'GATT-compatible' failed and, in the event, following a complaint by five Latin American banana-producing countries, a GATT panel has condemned it, and both the Latin American and the ACP exporters feel aggrieved by the new arrangements. While the eventual outcome of the banana dispute may depend on the GATT decision on the special trade preferences of the Lomé Convention (see below), neither the dispute nor its likely resolution arose in any direct way from the Uruguay Round. For that reason we do not deal in any greater depth with bananas. They are included in our estimates of the effects of the agreement, since they are subject to UR decisions on tariffs, but as a component of the 'other tropical goods' category.

Close to 100 % of goods 'originating' in the ACP states are granted preferential access in the EU market. The rules of origin are still a limit, although the smallest can obtain derogations from these. The access, unlike GSP, is contractual, and guaranteed for 10 years, the life of the current Convention (at present, to expire in 2000).

The role of ACP preferences in the past is difficult to measure. Through a comprehensive study of detailed ACP export data McQueen and Stevens (1989) identified a set of 'non-traditional' products where 'there has been an encouragingly rapid growth of ACP exports of new commodities'. But the results could be interpreted in different ways. McQueen and Stevens (1989) interpreted them (including those on agricultural products) as evidence of the value of preferences and of further potential, though they admitted that, within their sample, there seemed to be little correlation between success and the depth of the preference margin. Measured in terms of non-traditional exports, where the major preference margins are found, the utilisation of the ACP scheme is still limited. Only 28 of the 70 ACP countries have used it for such exports, and only 10 of these regularly (Marville, 1994).

Another set of developing country preferences that will be eroded by the UR are those granted by the United States under the CBI and a similar set granted under Canada's CARIBCAN. Under the Caribbean Basin Economic Recovery Act (CBERA) of 1990, which extended the original 1983 Act, Caribbean countries enjoy tariff- and quota-free access to the US market for all goods, subject to a short but critical list of exceptions. The most important of these are most textiles and apparel, some leather goods including footwear, petroleum and petroleum products, canned tuna and certain agricultural products. Sugar exports are subject to US quotas which vary from year to year.

Unlike the US GSP (and indeed the Lomé Convention), the CBI is not time-limited and so is more likely to stimulate foreign direct investment. The CBI allows for cumulation to meet the rules of origin whereas the GSP does not, and there is no graduation from it. The main products benefiting are beef, pineapples, frozen concentrated orange juice, rum, ethyl alcohol and raw cane sugar. In recent years the share of manufactured goods has risen at the expense of food and raw materials. The most important of the manufactures has been apparel. The high duties on apparel explain why the USITC estimates of duty forgone through the CBI have risen faster than CBI imports. The average duty saved on CBI imports was 4.33% in 1986 and 8.16% in 1990 (USITC 1991).

Normal textile and apparel items are not included in the CBERA scheme. However, under the tariff head HS 9802-00-60 and 9802-00-80 (previously known as 806.30 and 807A), metal articles made of US metals and articles of apparel which have been made out of textiles formed and woven in the United States are subject to duty only on the value added outside the US. Only in the case of apparel is this derogation used substantially. and, in that sector, it is of strategic significance for the Dominican Republic and Jamaica.

Of the total imports from CBI beneficiary countries, in 1990, 65.8% entered duty-free (USITC 1991). Of this, 26.2% were duty-free under MFN, 13.6% were classified as duty-free under the CBI and 6.3% under the GSP, though in some cases the allocation between the last two groups is arbitrary. Products that gained their duty-free status entirely under the CBI include beef, sugar, cigars, orange juice, tobacco and iron and steel bars. Another 15.3% were duty-free under HS 9802-00-60 and 9802-00-80 – offshore production using US inputs – while a further 4.5% entered duty-free under other special rate provisions.

Despite the apparent success of the CBI, the preferences are in fact significantly underutilised. The share of products that entered duty-free under the CBI was only 47.9% of the eligible imports in 1990, though the denominator includes some goods that might have entered duty-free under the GSP. If all duty-free imports under the GSP are omitted from the denominator the CBI utilisation rate is still only 61.3%. Thus in effect the take-up rate for the CBI is only between 50 and 60%.

Conclusions

Although developing countries are still concerned to protect the preferences which they have (cf. OAU, 1994: 'to safeguard commitments already entered into' and 'to avoid the erosion of acquired rights of developing countries in the GATT negotiations'), their approval of the Uruguay Round settlement and the general absence of strong complaints about preference erosion suggest that preferences are no longer seen as essential, or perhaps as achievable. The ASEAN countries accept the EU's target of eventually graduating them (although with reservations about the use of EU-determined criteria for 'developed' and about how 'gradually'). GATT's own conclusion (Seade, 1994) is that 'the regular GSP schemes are so circumscribed in most granting countries – subject to quota limitations, exclusion of products and conditions for countries to participate – that the increased certainty provided by reductions in bound MFN duties often more than compensates for the reduced margins of preference – apart from the fact that, of course, preference-giving countries are free to compensate for reduced preference margins by expanding the scope of GSP programs', but too much weight should not be attached to this as GATT has always questioned its usefulness. On the ACP, GATT's verdict is that, although 'ACP preferences tend to be less circumscribed than most GSP schemes...the compensating factor will still exist of having a greater security of market access under bound MFN tariffs...over the longer run'(*ibid*).

As well as the economic erosion, preference schemes are under threat from tighter interpretation of the rules on regional arrangements. Schemes restricted to developing countries remain less restricted than those for developed countries. The rules for the latter have been tightened, and the increasing number of developed-developing country schemes will need to meet fixed timetables and supervision of their progress to full free trade. A GATT working party has recently found that the Lomé Convention may be in breach of even present rules (the WTO provision is tighter) on legitimate derogations from MFN treatment. It is neither reciprocal (and thus allowable as a step towards a free trade area) nor general for all developing countries (and thus allowable under the provision for differential treatment). Without a clearer definition of 'developing country' and some limits on the extensions or withdrawals of privileges by non-economic criteria, it is easy to see how other schemes could be similarly challenged, especially if a tit-for-tat dispute between the US and EU developed. NAFTA will be examined in 1995; AFTA (in South-east Asia) may be later. Even Mercosur (Argentina, Brazil, Paraguay and Uruguay) has been brought under the tighter rules.

3. Agriculture

Background and model

Ideally a highly-disaggregated model is needed to assess the effects of the improvements in market access on the developing countries, and on particular countries and groups. It would take into account the various trade preferences enjoyed by certain groups of countries on certain industrialised markets. It would adjust for interdependencies in demand for and in the supply of different commodities. It would permit the dynamic effects of trade changes on growth and investment to be quantified and assessed. No such model exists. However, in conjunction with the OECD Development Centre, we were able to use their general equilibrium RUNS (Rural-Urban, North-South) model to simulate the effects of the Uruguay Round agreement, particularly for temperate agricultural goods – meats, grains and sugar.

Unfortunately the model cannot be used for other commodities. As the authors accept (Goldin et al., 1993), although they use it and quote its results for all trade, it is primarily designed for agricultural goods: 15 of the 20 commodities into which trade is disaggregated are agricultural and a 16th is fertilisers. Of the remaining four, only two are traded goods (the others are energy and services), and of these probably only 'other manufactures' are important exports for developing countries (the last is 'equipment goods', apparently meaning goods used in investment). This design reflects its origin as a model to estimate the effects of various agricultural liberalisation proposals. It is unsuitable for modelling effects of trade policy on world trade in all sectors because agricultural goods are less than 20% of total developing country exports, and a smaller share of world trade. It also excludes changes in non-tariff barriers (including the MFA) and in services, so that we can use it for only one of the three main changes in the Uruguay Round. (GATT's own estimates for developing countries (GATT, 1993 *developing*) are also unusable as they assume a completely proportional adjustment of GSP which, as discussed above, is not expected and would not be part of the Uruguay Round if it were, and make no allowance for quotas or other preferences.)

The OECD model has no provisions for differential tariffs and thus cannot cope with trade preferences. In order to assess trade diversion between different groups of developing countries and between the developing countries and the Western industrialised countries, we had recourse to partial equilibrium (p.e.) calculations with all their limitations – lack of demand and supply interdependencies and no feedback through factor markets. P.e. analysis estimates the direct effect of a change in one or more tariff rates on imports from alternative sources on the basis of assumptions about the elasticities of supply and demand. We used such models constrained by RUNS world price results for coffee and cocoa. Otherwise we used them independently for all products where the Round produced significant tariff changes for developing country exports.[3]

Our eclectic methodology cannot yield demonstrably consistent results. Taking only one good at a time, the p.e. models follow trade theory and common sense in predicting positive price effects for exports of tropical and industrial products from the reduction in trade barriers but falls in previously protected markets. However, since the Round reached an agreement on reductions in trade barriers over a broad range of goods and services, clearly negative price changes could arise from substitution and income effects on those goods where liberalisation

---

3. A full explanation of the methods used is available from Michael Davenport.

removed (relatively) small barriers or where they were non-existent (most primary products) and which we have not specifically modeled.[4] Nevertheless, our methods should at least identify the principal effects of the market access negotiations, and the main thrust of their differential implications for different groups of developing countries.

The United States resisted the formula approach to tariff-cutting, used in recent Rounds, and negotiations were conducted through 'offer and response' dialogue between an importing country and its principal supplying countries. In the case of agriculture, however, the core agreement established average and minimum reductions in import barriers and domestic and export subsidies which substantially constrained the offers on individual products.

ACP preferences

The three main instruments of preference for the ACP countries in EU agricultural trade are: exemption from tariffs, subject, for certain fruits and vegetables to the marketing timetable; reductions (of about 50%) in the variable levy, though in many cases subject to tariff quotas, on maize, millet, sorghum and rice, poultrymeat, pigmeat and dairy products; and specific quotas for beef and sugar. For most CAP products tariffs are small and are used to supplement variable levies. Tariffication could change this picture. If variable levies and other border measures are to be replaced by tariffs and if the ACP were to continue to enjoy tariff-free entry, their measured preferential margins would be greatly enhanced, although the actual effect would depend on how precisely the new tariffs reproduced the effect of the previous quotas. However the Lomé Convention only requires that the ACP States be granted more favourable treatment than other non-EU countries. One compromise solution would be to maintain the nominal preferential margin of, in most cases, about 50%. The agreement could therefore lead either to some modest erosion or to enhancement of existing preferences on CAP goods. We have chosen to assume that the *volumes* of the main ACP exports of CAP goods – beef, sugar and rice – will remain unaffected by the agreement. The assumptions regarding the prices received on preferential exports of these products are detailed in the following paragraphs.

The specific quotas on ACP boneless beef and veal are designed to help traditional suppliers by offering a 90% reduction in the variable levy. They appear to reflect aspiration rather than effective limits; at present they are not filled. The main effect of liberalisation will therefore be on ACP export prices. On existing exports under the scheme, ACP producers receive an economic rent equivalent to 90% of the variable levy which was equivalent to nearly 60% of the EU internal price in the 1986–88 base period. A reduction in the levy – or tariff – consistent with a 36% reduction in protection would mean a cut of some 9% in the rent received by the ACP suppliers plus whatever was the fall in the internal EU price. We assumed a total reduction in the price received by the ACP exporters of 18%.

Under the Sugar Protocol to Lomé IV the EU guarantees to buy specific quantities from

---

4. Substitution effects arise where consumers switch between goods in response to changes in relative prices, thereby bringing about second-order price changes. Income effects result from changes in real incomes effected by the initial changes in prices. Where incomes are reduced because of first-order price increases, consumers may buy less of other goods and bring about reductions in their prices.

27

particular ACP states at a fixed price. This is negotiated annually, but in the past it has closely followed the price guaranteed to EU sugar-beet growers. A significant fall in internal prices would be reflected in the price paid for ACP sugar. We assume an 11% fall in the price paid to both, leading to a major drop in revenues for the ACP countries, only marginally compensated by higher revenues from other sugar exports receiving the expected rise in the world sugar price of just over 5%. (For a discussion of the intricacies of the EU sugar regime and its post-Uruguay Round implications for the Protocol sugar exporters, see Woodward, 1994).

Under Annex 40 of Lomé IV the ACP states have a preference in their exports of rice to the EU of a 50% reduction in the import levy together with a specific Ecu reduction depending on the nature of the rice, Ecu 0.36 for paddy and husked rice, Ecu 0.54 for wholly milled rice and Ecu 0.30 for broken rice[5] all up to a maximum of 125,000 tonnes of husked rice equivalent and 20,000 tonnes of broken rice. Among the Commonwealth Caribbean countries only Guyana is a significant exporter of rice. But already there are complaints from Guyana and Suriname – also a major rice exporter – that present rice quotas are insufficient.

In principle the tariffication of levies will mean that the first and most significant part of this preference – the reduction in levies by 50% – is lost. In fact, one can assume that the percentage reduction applies to the new tariffs – probably adjusted so that the fixed Ecu amount does not result in an increase in the value of the preference as the tariffs are cut. In practice, it is assumed in this report that the preferences of the ACP producers remain such as to prevent any trade shift to or from third country producers.

The ACP rice producers will, however, still experience a price effect on their exports to the EU. At present they receive a price roughly half-way between the world price and the CAP intervention price. The UR agreement is likely to leave the world price largely unaffected – we actually assume an increase of 0.9% – but there will probably be a significant fall in the EU price as border protection and internal subsidies are reduced. Here, a fall in the EU price of 20% relative to the world price, or 19% in absolute terms and a reduction in the prices received by ACP producers of 9.5% on the quantity exported to the EU in the GATT base period, 1986–88, is assumed.

One path to increasing the value-added of exports may be through the processing of domestic primary products. In coffee, cocoa, sisal and other agaves, and in non-coniferous wood, the share of exports undergoing even the most basic processing is still extremely small (Davenport and Stevens, 1990). McQueen and Stevens (1989) identify a few ACP countries which had expanded their exports in a limited number of products, canned tuna (Côte d'Ivoire, Senegal, Fiji, Mauritius, Solomons, Ghana, Seychelles), leather accessories (Mauritania, Ethiopia), wood products (Cameroon, Congo, Côte d'Ivoire, Ghana, Zaïre). The extent to which the tariff advantage in processed products helped these countries is difficult to say without a product-by-product investigation. In some cases the main competitors were probably receiving the same tariff-free access under the GSP.

---

5. For semi-milled rice the reduction is ajdusted by the component for the protection of the UE milling industry.

The limited progress that many developing countries, including the ACP states, have made in moving downstream is doubly unfortunate to the extent that their tariff preferences through the GSP and through Lomé on the EU market have generally been greater the higher the level of processing, and that this advantage of being exempted from tariff escalation will now be eroded. One of the results of the Tokyo Round of multilateral trade negotiations was, for many of the exports of the developing countries, an increase in tariff escalation. In the Uruguay Round, in the two important cases of coffee and cocoa, the reduction of EU MFN tariffs on beans to zero will inevitably mean increased escalation.

GATT (1993 *developing*) presents a table, reproduced as Table 3.1, showing changes in escalation for selected product categories. Of the thirteen product categories considered, tariffs both before and after the Round increase with processing, in all except wood and paper. Of the eleven products which display tariff escalation, the Round will definitely reduce that escalation in tobacco, copper, nickel, aluminium, and tin. Where there are several different stages of processing there may be escalation between certain stages and not between others higher up the chain. But on balance escalation is probably reduced in hides and leather, rubber and jute. In the cases of zinc it is increased.

The tariff rates in the table take no account of GSP concessions. Most GSP schemes – leather, wood and tobacco being exceptions – allow zero-tariff entry for goods at different stages of processing, in which case tariff escalation is only a problem where the GSP is not utilised. With utilisation rates at about 50%, escalation may still be a problem for the developing countries, even in the metals and metal goods sectors, but a rather more complex one that the table suggests.

Effects on trade in temperate agricultural products

The principal features of the agreement in agriculture are:

- The 'tariffication' of non-tariff border barriers. Initially the tariffs will be designed to provide substantially the same level of protection[6] but they are to be reduced by an average 36% on the 1986–88 base period, with a minimum reduction of 15% for each tariff line over six years, or by 24% over 10 years for developing countries. Minimum access tariff quotas (at reduced tariff rates) are established where current imports consti- tute less than 3% of domestic consumption. These quotas are to be expanded to 5% over the implementation period. 'Special safeguard' mechanisms are available to meet import 'surges', closely defined in terms of penetration rates. A 'special treatment' clause allows countries to maintain import restrictions to the end of the implementation period where imports have been minor, export subsidies have not been provided, production is restricted and specific minimum access opportunities are made available. The EU and some other countries have chosen to use specific rather than *ad valorem* duties, ensuring that revenue will not be directly affected by price changes. Quantitative restrictions for

---

6. In principle, this is impossible: the equivalence of any tariff and a quota or other absolute limit can only hold for a particular set of conditions of supply and demand, and emprically even calculating it for a particular base (as required here) is dependent on all the modelling difficulties already discussed. The actual levels notified have probably been set to give a protective margin for error, and some have been over 200% (Agosin, *et al.*, 1994).

Table 3.1 Changes in tariff escalation in selected product categories

Product category by stage of processing	Weighted average			Change in tariff escalation
	Pre-	Post-	Reduction	
Hides, skins and leather				
raw	0.1	0.1	0	n.a.
semi-manufactures	4.6	3.6	22	-22
finished products	8.7	7.0	20	-20
total	5.2	4.1	21	n.a.
Rubber				
raw	0.1	0	100	n.a.
semi-manufactures	5.5	3.3	40	-39
finished products	5.1	3.6	30	-28
total	3.4	2.3	32	n.a.
Wood				
in the rough	0.0	0	0	n.a.
panels	9.4	6.5	31	-30
semi-manufactures	0.9	0.4	50	-50
articles	4.7	1.6	67	-67
total	2.0	1.1	43	n.a.
Paper				
pulp	0.0	0	0	n.a.
paper etc.	5.3	0	100	-100
printed matter	1.7	0.3	83	-83
paper articles	7.3	0	100	-100
total	3.5	0	99	n.a.
Jute				
fibres	0.0	0	0	n.a.
yarns	5.4	0.1	98	-98
fabrics	5.7	3.2	43	-43
total	5.1	1.8	64	n.a.
Copper				
unwrought	0.9	0.7	30	n.a.
semi-manufactures	4.3	3.1	28	-28
total	1.7	1.2	39	n.a.
Nickel				
unwrought	0.5	0.3	40	n.a.
semi-manufactures	2.6	1.0	63	-68
total	0.7	0.4	48	n.a.
Aluminium				
unwrought	2.1	1.6	23	n.a.
semi-manufactures	5.9	4.8	17	-14
total	3.0	2.4	20	n.a.
Lead				
unwrought	2.4	1.3	45	n.a.
semi-manufactures	4.5	2.8	37	-29
total	2.4	1.4	44	n.a.
Zinc				
unwrought	2.1	1.8	17	n.a.
semi-manufactures	4.7	2.9	38	-56
total	2.2	1.8	19	n.a.
Tin				
unwrought	0.1	0	100	n.a.
semi-manufactures	3.9	1.8	53	-53
total	0.1	1.1	53	n.a.
Tobacco				
unmanufactured	14.7	11.5	22	n.a.
manufactured	22.1	9.2	58	-131
total	17.3	10.7	38	n.a.

Notes: (i) Tariff escalation is defined as the wedge between the processed and the unprocessed or raw product. The percentage change in tariff escalation is calculated as the decline in the tariff wedge divided by the original wedge. (ii) 'n.a.' means 'not applicable'.

Source: GATT (1993 developing)

balance-of-payments purposes in developing countries are not subject to tariffication, but their tariffs must be bound and reduced in the same manner as other tariffs.

- Minimum access tariff quotas are to be established of a size sufficient to bring imports up to 5% of domestic consumption, e.g. if imports currently account for 4% of domestic consumption, a tariff quota equivalent to 1% must be established.

- Domestic support to the agricultural sector is to be reduced by 20% on the same base years and over the same transition period or by 13.3% for developing countries, subject to a number of exclusions. These include *de minimis* provisions below which the rules do not apply – where imports are less than 5% of production, 10% in the case of developing countries, and where the measures are deemed to have minimal trade-distorting effects (see below).

- Export subsidies are to be reduced to a level 36% below the 1986–90 base and the quantity of subsidized exports by 21%, both over the same implementation period. Under the 'front loading' provisions, a country can start subsidy reductions from the 1991–92 levels, where these are higher than the 1986–90 base levels, though the end point of the reductions is unchanged. For developing countries the reductions are to be two thirds those applying to the developed countries. In all cases, trade barriers, domestic support measures and export subsidies are closely defined.

- The new tariffs and reduced levels of domestic support are also now all 'bound' in GATT terms, as discussed in Chapter 2.

The instruments to be reduced and restricted include price-support policies, income-support policies linked to production, or other subsidies discriminating against imports. Those to be 'bound' in the GATT sense and subject to negotiated reductions include investment grants and subsidized loans.

Measures judged to have a minimal effect on trade, the so-called 'green box', are excluded from the reduction commitments. In particular, income-support policies not linked to – in the jargon those 'decoupled from' – output would be permitted, as would environmental programmes and domestic food aid. Certain assistance measures to promote agricultural and rural development in developing countries are also allowed. Direct payments under production-limiting programmes, the so-called 'blue box', are broadly exempt from reduction. A set of 'peace' provisions was also agreed. These include an agreement that action, including countervailing duty measures, available under the Subsidies Agreement would not be applied to green box policies.

Table 3.2 gives the reductions in tariffs and/or tariff equivalents of NTBs offered by the developed countries by product group, calculated by the participants in the manner agreed in the negotiations. (These are not changes in the absolute level.) The package is likely to affect world prices and the pattern of trade in those goods where protection among the Western industrialised countries has been high – grains, in particular wheat, but also rice and coarse grains, 'red' meats (beef, sheepmeat and pig meat), dairy products and sugar. This will happen mainly through the reductions in exports of these products by the Western countries, though the minimum access provisions may also be important in certain commodities, e.g.

Table 3.2: Tariff and tariff-equivalent reductions by developed economies on agricultural product categories (US $ million and %)

Product categories	Value of imports	% reduction in tariffs
Coffee, tea, cocoa, sugar etc.	13,634	34
Fruits and vegetables	14,575	36
Oilseeds, fats and oils	12,584	40
Other agricultural products	15,585	48
Animals and products	9,596	32
Beverages and spirits	6,608	39
Flowers, plants, vegetable materials	1,945	48
Tobacco	3,086	36
Grains	5,310	39
Dairy products	1,317	26
All agricultural products	84,240	37

Source: GATT, 1994 *Access*

cheese and rice.

The developing countries will also be affected through their own obligations under the agreement, although as noted above these are limited by special provisions. Most ACP states, being in the category of least developed countries, are not required to reduce their tariffs at all and the obligations to reduce export subsidies do not apply to them, although the binding requirements would do so if any had been notified to GATT (none has).

There has been little consensus about the effects of the package on trade in temperate agricultural goods. This is partly because of the different models and partly because different researchers have made different assumptions about what the agreement might actually achieve. Our calculations with the RUNS model used the actual agreements in the Final Act.[7] Even

---

7. Neither time nor the limited availability of the full final offers allowed us to introduce detailed changes in tariff and non-tariff barriers for each product and for each country or country group. Instead the model was fed the average requirements specified in the Final Act (and outlined above). The export subsidy commitments have to be met product by product. In the case of tariff cuts, the implicit assumption made here is that the average required cuts will in general be applied across the board. As well as the specified average tariff cuts, there is a minimum reduction in tariffs of 15% across all goods. It is possible, therefore, to make only the minimum cut

then there were major problems in assigning specific liberalisation moves to the Uruguay Round. The 1992 CAP reform was undertaken partly in order to anticipate some of the likely requirements of an agreement. But there was also considerable budgetary pressure for reform in both the EU and the US. If the Eastern European countries were admitted to the EU, their financial assistance requirements could be large, putting further budgetary pressure on the EU to take action equivalent to, if not beyond, what the Uruguay settlement requires. In Japan, opening the rice market to imports was in part the result of long-term constraints on supply, aggravated by a poor harvest in 1993. South Africa believes that it has met its obligations on reducing subsidies already, and that it can now gain on exports. Clearly it is impossible to attribute a specific share to the Uruguay Round. We have simulated the full Final Act requirements, even though, not only in the EU but also in the US and many developing countries, those requirements are largely already implemented. (This is taken into account in Chapter 6 where we estimate how soon the effects of the UR will appear.)

Our assumption then can be regarded as giving an upper limit to the effects. The world price and trade flow changes in agricultural goods that we attribute to the UR are the results of the reduction in protection – whether in the form of border tariffs and other barriers, of subsidies to the domestic farm sector or subsidies to exports – between the base period and the end of the transition period. In other words, we attribute any reduction in the instruments of protection, relative to their UR base period levels, even if it has already taken place, to the Uruguay Round. Clearly there have been other factors at work, in particular the exigencies of national budgets in the developed countries, including the EU, the requirements of structural adjustment programmes agreed with the IMF or the World Bank in the case of many developing countries, even simply convictions about the gains from liberalisation in a number of both these categories of countries. Nevertheless, in most cases the simultaneous negotiations of the Uruguay Round played a critical role in strengthening the hand of the free traders, not only in lowering barriers to trade and reducing the degree of internal subsidisation, but also in the choice of acceptable policy instruments.

The results of the simulation are summarised in Table 3.3.[8] These are the final, 'steady

---

on the main imports and much larger cuts on non-traditional imports, as the formula is a simple average of the percentage, not absolute cuts. The analytically indefensible use of percentage changes in percentage rates will permit further manipulation by giving large cuts on low tariffs. Without knowing the details of each offer at each stage, it is impossible to know how this affects the results, but it is probable that the average cut used here will overestimate the effects, especially in the most sensitive goods, except in countries which would be making the compulsory cuts on their own initiative. It would be possible for the average to be not much more than the compulsory 15%, half what is assumed here.

8.   The RUNS (Rural-Urban North-South) model disaggregates agricultural production and trade into the commodity groups mentioned above and into 22 countries or regions, with labour inputs and investment in each sector endogenous, though for each country or region net international capital flows were constrained to predetermined, generally expanding, paths over the ten-year simulation horizon. Total savings, including foreign savings (net capital flow), are allocated to investment in the rural and urban sectors. Market distortions – and national policies – are incorporated through domestic-international price 'wedges' and measures of input subsidies in each sector. These are based on OECD and USDA calculations of producer subsidy equivalents. A base case simulation is used to check the plausibility of the sectoral output and macroeconomic variables, though productivity gains are exogenous and the key element to growth is capital accumulation. The labour force is exogenous. Details about the RUNS model and discussions of earlier simulations can be found in Goldin *et al* (1993).

Table 3.3: Temperate agricultural products, price changes and net exports as a share of demand in the base and Uruguay Round simulations (%).

	wheat		rice		coarse grains		sugar		beef, sheep		other meats		oils		dairy	
change in price base run (no UR)	-8.9		12.7		-27.3		n.a.[(c)]		5.2		-1.9		-12.8		8.4	
assumed change in price with UR	-6.3		12.6		-26.4		n.a.[(c)]		7.9		-2.4		-12.5		14.6	
change in price because of UR effects	3.6		0.9		1.9		5.2		3.7		0.5		1.3		7.2	
	(a)	(b)	(a)	(b)	(a)	(b)	(a)	(b)	(a)	(b)	(a)	(b)	(a)	(b)	(a)	(b)
Nigeria	-73	-74	10	7	-52	-49	-78	-77	-20	-15	-38	-36	-67	-64	-55	-52
India	-9	-8	14	15	-23	-21	8	16	11	15	17	17	-1	-1	18	24
Brazil	-45	-47	73	62	10	6	6	17	4	10	5	9	38	42	6	14
Mexico	-52	-55	-41	-40	-51	-55	-15	-8	107	120	-45	-48	-81	-80	-26	-21
China (PRC)	-27	-24	-11	-10	30	33	2	10	165	176	8	10	-35	-32	12	21
Indonesia	-100	-100	21	22	20	25	-32	-36	-10	-6	66	71	16	5	-28	-22
Africa	-70	-70	-32	-32	-33	-32	9	8	-13	-9	-27	-25	-40	-41	-13	-8
Latin America	-24	-24	80	49	-22	-25	33	42	16	21	-8	-7	20	24	-2	5
South Asia	-13	-11	10	10	-23	-20	2	10	10	13	8	9	-16	-14	16	21
Other Asia	-30	-27	-7	-6	25	27	5	8	104	108	6	9	-20	-20	13	18
Developing countries total	-32	-30	-1	-1	-6	-6	8	12	21	25	4	6	-12	-11	0	5

(a) net exports as % of utilisation in base (without UR)
(b) net exports as % total utilisation with Uruguay Round
(c) as explained in the text, these assumptions were modified.

Country groups (this table only)
Africa: Sub-Saharan excluding South Africa
Latin America: includes Caribbean
South Asia: Afghanistan, Bangladesh, Bhutan, Burma, India, Kampuchea, Korea (DR), Laos, Maldives, Mongolia, Nepal, Pakistan, Sri Lanka, Viet Nam
Other Asia: Brunei, China PRC, Fiji, Fr. Polynesia, Hong Kong, Indonesia, Korea (rep. of), Macao, Malaysia, New Caledonia, New Hebrides, Papua New Guinea, Philippines, Singapore, Taiwan, Thailand, Tonga

Sources: see text.

state', effects. They measure the differences between the projected values, given the assumed 'base' changes in price, and those under the Uruguay Round settlement after all the lags have worked out.

The predicted price changes, relative to those of the base simulation, are modest compared with some of the numbers which have been produced, but not very far from GATT's own most recent estimate, an average rise of 5% (Seade, 1994). As the EU, US and other offers have already been implemented through reduced domestic subsidies and cuts in border protection, to some extent the price increases in Table 3.3 would take place even without a settlement. Furthermore our simulations assume full price transmission; all changes in international prices are reflected in farmgate prices and retail prices. Clearly if some countries follow a policy of insulating urban consumers from increases in world prices, and decline to pass them on to the farm sector, overall demand will be higher and supply lower than estimated by the model. This would mean that the model underestimates changes in world agricultural policies. In general, we assume that these two principal sources of bias cancel one another out.

The predictions on changes in the supply-demand balances reveal considerable variability depending on the region/country and product.[9] The statistics presented are net exports of each commodity as a share in domestic consumption, with and without the Uruguay Round liberalisation. Thus an increase indicates a rise in net exports or reduction in net imports.

In wheat the effect is estimated as raising the ratio of net exports to consumption by some 3 percentage points; in rice and coarse grains the effects are minimal, while in sugar and dairy products there is a significant increase in net exports. Consumption of vegetable oils falls with dairy products replacing them.

The Effects on Net Food Importing Countries and the Ministerial Declaration

In general the developing countries experience real net export rises from the higher prices they receive from exports or have to pay on imported foods. On balance they are food-importing countries so these net export gains may translate into welfare losses. A Committee on Agriculture (within the WTO) will estimate the cost to the food importers and, under the Decision on Measures concerning the Possible Negative Effects of the Reform Programme on Least Developed and Net Food-Importing Developing Countries, report to the WTO ministerial meeting, making recommendations, if appropriate, for food aid and/or compensatory finance from bilateral or multilateral sources. There will also be a Unit for the least developed. The recommendations have no formal mechanism for implementation as the WTO itself has no food or funds. This decision raises several practical and conceptual issues. It is not clear how the estimate will be made. The range of estimates *a priori* of Uruguay Round effects on agricultural prices and countries' volume responses indicates that there could be a wide band of uncertainty; it is the change attributable to the Round not the observed change which is the criterion; the latter could be positive or negative (as we have seen in Table 3.3). The bilateral donors could (the EU apparently already does) take this clause as a possible justification for continuing subsidised food aid; this is the principal remedy which the Decision stresses, and it would be permissible under the Food Aid Convention in spite of the restrictions on agricultural subsidies. The multilateral organisations, who are said to be 'sympathetic' to the proposal, could make any assistance conditional, on economic or other policies. This would be different from the conventional assumption of an absolute right to compensation under other GATT provisions. This is the only example of GATT or WTO supporting compensation for a loss of benefit through general liberalisation rather than

---

9. For temperate products, for which developing countries are both exporters and importers, the effects can appear as changes in exports or imports. For this reason, net trade is used. For other sectors, the effects are largely on exports (any import effects from their own tariff reductions are assumed to have alreadty gone through), so that the tables show changes in these. The effects on trade among developing countries are discussed at the end of Chapter 4.

through protection; the nearest parallel is the compensation payable to third countries in the case of the formation of a regional trading group, but this is different because a regional group is not an unambiguous move toward greater multilateral liberalisation.

But the whole pattern of negotiation in agriculture was very different from the traditional product-by-product exporter against importer form. One conflict of interests was between the exporters (the US and EC) which wanted to maintain trade barriers and other exporters (the Cairns group),[10] which wanted to lower them. A second, also between exporters, was between different degrees and forms of protection; this was between the US and EC. Food importers also eventually formed a group to protect their interests. But because of the past distortions these importers' interests were actually in continued distortion, and therefore in protection. This unusual situation is evidence of limitations on the approach used by GATT (and in this report) of looking only at perceived national interests: producers in the importing countries would have an interest in higher prices, and consumers in the protecting exporters in lower prices.

The upper-income countries of Asia and the Gulf region and South Africa increase their consumption of most products more than their output. But for all products (except vegetable oils) in most countries or regions, output rises more than demand. The output increases will be concentrated in the main producing countries. China and Latin America (as a whole) are major producers of all the products, India of cereals, dairy products, sugar and oils, Africa of meat and oils, the Mediterranean of oils. These regions will significantly increase supply if, as the model run presumes, the world price increases are fully passed on to the farmers.

In addition to the effects of the overall changes in world prices and trade flows, ACP exports will be harmed by the erosion of their complex set of preferences on temperate agricultural products. Of these the most important are the beef and sugar protocols under which the EU has agreed to buy specific quantities of beef and sugar from particular countries each year through the duration of the Lomé Convention. In sugar, the main beneficiaries are Mauritius, Fiji, Guyana, Jamaica and Swaziland. In 1992 they exported some 1600 tonnes, more than half as much again as their combined quota of 1040 tonnes. We assume that the reduction in the EU price *per se* will not affect the tonnage of exports to the EU, i.e. that it remains sufficiently high for the quota holders to want to fill their quotas. The loss of economic rent is still substantial, some US $39 million in the case of Mauritius and $14 million for Fiji. To some extent these losses are compensated by higher prices on sales to other markets. This is the case particularly for Fiji.

In beef the situation is rather different. The benefiting countries have by no means exploited their quotas. Even Botswana, the major beneficiary, exported only 16,700 tonnes in 1992 out of a quota of 18,900. Nevertheless, in Botswana's case beef and veal exports under Protocol 7 represented over 60% of the country's total exports to the EU. The loss to Botswana is estimated at $ 11.6 million.

---

10. Argentina, Bangladesh, Brazil, China, Colombia, Dominican Republic, Egypt, El Salvador, Guatemala, Hong Kong, India, Indonesia, Jamaica, Macau, Malaysia, Singapore, South Korea, Sri Lanka, Thailand, Uruguay, and Yugoslavia.

Table 3.4: Temperate agricultural products, changes in net exports based on 1990 data, (US $ m)

	Net exports, $ million av. 1990-92			Final UR effect change in net exports, $ m.				Net exports $ mill.	
	Meat, dairy (a)	Grains inc oil seeds	Sugar	Meat, dairy	Grains inc oil seeds	Sugar	Total	pre-UR	post-UR
Angola	-129	-90	-35	-7.2	-2.0	-1.5	-10.7	-254	-265
Botswana	67	-26	-27	-11.3	-0.6	-1.1	-13.1	14	1
Cameroon	-17	-91	-3	-1.0	-2.2	-0.1	-3.3	-111	-114
Côte d'Ivoire	-75	-166	1	-4.2	-3.8	0.2	-7.7	-240	-248
Ethiopia	-11	-157	3	-0.6	-3.5	0.2	-3.9	-165	-169
Ghana	-43	-74	-42	-2.4	-1.6	-1.8	-5.9	-159	-164
Kenya	1	-62	-37	-0.2	-1.5	-2.0	-3.7	-99	-102
Malawi	-4	-57	28	-0.2	-1.3	-0.2	-1.7	-33	-35
Mauritius	-57	-52	363	-3.2	-1.2	-24.1	-28.5	254	226
Mozambique	-13	-137	-4	-0.7	-3.1	0.0	-3.8	-154	-158
Nigeria	-70	-174	-155	-3.0	-4.0	-10.4	-17.4	-399	-416
Senegal	-50	-150	-21	-2.9	-3.4	-0.9	-7.2	-222	-229
Somalia	-3	-66	-5	-0.2	-1.4	-0.2	-1.8	-74	-76
Sudan	-19	-67	4	-1.0	-2.3	0.3	-3.0	-82	-85
Tanzania	-3	-29	-3	-0.3	-0.8	-1.0	-2.1	-35	-37
Zambia	-1	-42	7	-0.1	-1.0	0.4	-0.6	-36	-36
Zimbabwe	14	-40	20	-6.2	-1.7	1.6	-6.3	-6	-12
Guyana	-8	11	98	-0.4	-0.6	-9.4	-10.4	101	91
Jamaica	-62	-96	66	-3.5	-2.5	-7.7	-13.7	-92	-106
Fiji	-19	-21	166	-0.5	1.0	-3.2	-2.7	127	124
Papua New Guinea	-70	-60	0	-1.9	2.5	0.2	0.9	-130	-129
ACP (57) (b)	-1041	-2716	627	-80.5	-61.7	-75.5	-217.7	-3130	-3347
Argentina	797	2281	127	13.3	76.3	5.3	94.9	3205	3300
Brazil	565	-391	560	-19.7	52.1	-2.8	29.6	734	763
Chile	-30	-53	-39	-2.7	-0.9	-3.1	-6.8	-121	-128
Colombia	12	-171	117	-0.2	-4.2	5.0	0.6	-43	-42
Mexico	-118	-148	-25	-6.6	2.8	-3.2	-7.0	-291	-298
Venezuela	-93	-295	-40	-5.8	-7.5	-3.2	-16.5	-428	-445
Bangladesh	-76	-238	-23	-4.2	-2.9	-2.1	-9.3	-337	-346
India	79	135	71	1.6	-0.1	0.7	2.2	285	287
Indonesia	-83	-635	-79	-3.3	-8.0	0.8	-10.4	-797	-807
Korea (Rep. of)	-470	-1686	-241	-13.1	54.1	5.9	46.9	-2397	-2350
Malaysia	-231	-646	-135	-6.7	26.4	4.5	24.3	-1012	-988
Thailand	245	1260	732	5.2	60.9	64.6	130.8	2237	2367
Africa	-1510	-3450	-270	-103.2	-78.6	-37.7	-219.5	-5230	-5449
Latin America	-470	-1351	4361	-114.8	-6.8	145.7	24.2	2540	2564
South Asia	-82	-229	-120	-7.6	-4.1	-20.4	-32.0	-432	-464
Other Asia	558	-410	38	-0.9	-219.3	8.9	-211.3	187	-25
ASEAN	-539	-1707	276	-17.8	133.4	75.9	191.5	-1970	-1778
Developing Countries (c)	-5791	-14479	2673	-373.3	-77.8	209.8	-241.3	-17596	-17837
Least Developed (d)	-446	-1929	-387	-40	-36.9	-29.6	-106.8	-2762	-2869

(a) live animals excluded as data insufficient; (b) the following ACP States were omitted from the calculations owing to lack of data: Sao Tome and Principe, Seychelles, Antigua and Barbuda, Bahamas, Dominica, St Kitts and Nevis, St Lucia, St Vincent, Kiribati, Samoa and Tuvalu; (c) excludes Taiwan. Other Asia includes Hong Kong, Singapore and Korea (Rep. of); (d) LDCs exclude Bhutan, Cape Verde, Djibouti, Equatorial Guinea, Kiribati, Myanmar, Samoa, Sao Tome and Principe

Source: see text

Estimates of the trade effects of the liberalisation of temperate agriculture are shown in Table 3.4. These are obtained by applying the regional supply-demand balance effects of Table 3.3 to the countries composing those groups and adding in the Lomé beef, rice and sugar effects. The final percentage effects are applied to average 1990–92 trade flows to indicate their relative magnitude. Net ACP exports are estimated to worsen by some $200 million, while for the developing countries as a whole they fall by about $250 million.

If the overall trade effects seem small, it is important to stress that there will be not only static but also dynamic effects. In principle these are already included in the estimates of the effects. But national policies can make all the difference. If higher world prices are not passed on to farmers, they would not lead to more investment in agriculture, to diversification in favour of newly-profitable crops and livestock and to an invigorated export sector. In the case of net food-importing countries, price signals can encourage the development of the indigenous agricultural sector.

It is also important to note that some apparently minor effects at the global level can be important to particular countries. Clearly this is the case in the loss of earnings on sugar for Mauritius for which exports to the EU under the Sugar Protocol are an important component of overall export earnings. As long as the price paid for ACP sugar remains tied to the EU intervention price, the ACP sugar producers will experience cuts in their export earnings. On the other hand the rise in world prices, about 5% is estimated, may allow certain ACP producers, including Jamaica, to sell on the world market.[11] There will of course be many other factors affecting the world price. Increased output in Eastern Europe and the former Soviet Union will have a negative effect. On the other hand the world price should be strengthened by the diversification out of sugar production of Cuba, which is the world's largest exporter but one that is generally uncompetigtive at world prices.

One modest but nonetheless positive effect of the UR agreement will be on the variability of world prices of temperate agricultural goods. The variability will decline as the Western industrialised countries reduce their dumping on the world market. At present these subsidized exports vary substantially in quantity from year to year, causing sharp fluctuations in overall world supply. As the share of supply on the world market outside protective schemes rises, random effects of weather (or policy shocks in any one country) will become less important. Anderson and Tyers (1990) estimated that instability would be reduced by almost half by 2000 in their phased 50% reduction simulation. The effects may be minor, but they will at least operate in the right direction.

The significance of protection for world price instability is not unchallenged. Duncan (1991) argues that instability arises primarily from speculative behaviour. This could increase as protection is reduced. However, he is primarily concerned with stockpiling effects. The use of futures and options markets would increase and that could be either stabilising or destabilising.

---

11. The most efficient estate factory in Jamaica, Worthy Park, can produce sugar at approximately 13 to 14 cents per lb. The production cost of the least efficient is now some 17 to 18 cents. The current world price is 12 cents plus, though this has been boosted by drought in some major growing countries. In due course with more investment in plant and irrigation, some of the other estates – now largely privatised – may also become competitive in the world market.

38

Trade in tropical products

Coffee and cocoa account for about three quarters of the value of imports from the developing countries of the products covered in the EU's offer.[12] Most Western industrialised countries allow tariff-free imports of tropical beverage crops – at least in their unprocessed state – but the EU has until now maintained tariffs on coffee and cocoa beans, though not on tea, to protect the preference margin of the ACP States. The Mid-Term offer (1988) reduced the MFN tariffs on coffee beans from 5.0% to 3.0% and eliminated the GSP rate which had been at 4.5%; these changes were implemented in 1991. The rate on cocoa beans was already 3.0%. The final offers bring the EU rates on coffee and cocoa beans down to zero. Table 3.5 shows the other pre- and post-Round MFN and GSP tariffs[13]. On tobacco and oilseeds as well, the EU maintains higher MFN tariffs than most OECD countries, again presumably to sustain the preference margins of the ACP.

Table 3.5: Tropical products and fish: OECD pre- and post-UR MFN and GSP tariff rates

		coffee beans	cocoa beans	tobacco	oilseeds oils	other tropical	fish
EU	MFN pre-UR	5.0	3.0	22.5	8.0	7.6	14.0
	MFN post-UR	0.0	0.0	17.8	5.1	4.2	12.0
	GSP pre-UR	4.5	-	22.2	2.5	6.0	10.6
	GSP post-UR	0.0	-	17.8	2.5	4.2	10.6
other	MFN pre-UR	0.0	0.0	10.0	4.0	9.0	3.7
OECD	MFN post-UR	0.0	0.0	5.0	2.5	5.7	1.1
	GSP pre-UR	-	-	0.0	1.0	0.5	0.0
	GSP post-UR	-	-	0.0	1.0	0.5	0.0

Sources: various national tariff schedules and UR offers; GATT, 1994 *Access.*

12. Tropical products here and in the Tropical Products Negotiating Group (TPNG) exclude products produced in the US or EU, such as rice, which were dealt with in the Agricultural Group. Tobacco and vegetable oils were also excluded from the TPNG but are included here, since tariff preferences are important and the RUNS model cannot deal with those. The two groups were later merged and all tropical agricultural products are governed by the Agreement on Agriculture.

13. Where under the EU GSP scheme tariff-quotas are exceeded – notably in tobacco – the GSP tariff for that sub-item is treated as equal to the MFN tariff because it no longer has the function of allocating EU imports to the GSP beneficiaries at the margin.

39

Table 3.6: Tropical products, changes in export revenues (US $m)

	coffee	cocoa	tobacco	veget. oils	other tropical	fish	OECD imports 1992	Volume change	change in value
Share in EU impts, %									
ACP	33.2	77.0	6.9	2.3	12.5	3.4			
other developing	66.8	23.0	6.3	20.3	12.4	24.6			
Developed countries	0.0	0.0	86.9	77.4	75.1	72.0			
Change in:									
world price	-1.5	-1.2	-1.9	0.9	1.4	0.9			
EU price	-3.8	-1.7	-2.7	-0.6	-1.5	-1.6			
Trade shift									
ACP (a)	1.5	0.5	2.8	1.1	2.3	1.7			
other developing (b)	-0.7	-1.7	-0.5	-0.1	-0.8	-0.1			
Trade creation (c)	0.7	0.1	2.0	1.0	1.7	1.5			
Angola	-0.3	0.0	0.0	0.0	0.0	-0.2	10.9	-0.2	-0.5
Botswana	0.0	0.0	0.0	0.0	0.0	0.0	0.0	0.0	0.0
Cameroon	-5.9	-1.4	-0.1	-0.2	-2.3	0.0	170.8	-3.9	-9.9
Côte d'Ivoire	-7.9	-9.8	0.0	-2.2	-10.4	-2.8	608.7	-15.7	-33.1
Ethiopia	-3.4	0.0	0.0	0.0	-0.1	0.0	88.4	-1.0	-3.5
Ghana	-0.1	-3.8	0.0	-0.1	-1.6	-0.7	61.2	-3.0	-6.1
Kenya	-7.6	0.0	-0.3	0.0	-11.6	-1.0	497.4	-10.2	-20.5
Malawi	-0.5	0.0	-16.6	0.0	-0.8	0.0	341.7	-9.7	-17.9
Mauritius	0.0	-0.1	0.0	0.0	-0.5	-0.6	40.2	-0.6	-1.1
Mozambique	0.0	0.0	-0.2	0.0	-0.6	0.0	19.4	-0.5	-0.8
Nigeria	0.0	-1.6	0.0	-0.3	-3.7	-0.1	103.8	-3.3	-5.8
Senegal	0.0	0.0	0.0	-1.4	-0.1	-2.6	157.9	-2.4	-4.1
Somalia	0.0	0.0	0.0	0.0	0.0	0.0	0.0	0.0	0.0
Sudan	0.0	0.0	0.0	-0.1	0.0	0.0	5.3	-0.1	-0.2
Tanzania	-3.4	0.0	-1.0	0.0	-0.7	0.0	114.1	-1.9	-5.2
Zambia	-0.1	0.0	-0.4	0.0	-0.1	0.0	14.0	-0.3	-0.7
Zimbabwe	-0.7	0.0	-13.8	0.0	-1.5	0.0	336.9	-8.3	-16.0
Guyana	0.0	0.0	0.0	0.0	0.0	-0.1	4.1	-0.1	-0.1
Jamaica	-0.2	0.0	-0.4	0.0	-0.6	0.0	37.1	-0.6	-1.2
Fiji	0.0	0.0	0.0	-0.1	-0.1	-0.7	31.9	-0.6	-1.0
Papua-New Guinea	-3.5	-0.5	0.0	-2.9	-0.3	0.0	189.5	-3.0	-7.2
ACP (66)	-54.8	-18.7	-37.9	-8.2	-43.2	-13.8	5159.8	-83.2	-176.7
Argentina	0.0	0.0	2.5	1.3	0.9	2.4	725.7	0.7	7.0
Brazil	6.2	2.9	13.3	0.5	8.7	0.3	2627.5	28.3	31.9
Chile	0.0	0.0	0.2	0.1	1.3	5.0	771.9	0.1	6.7
Colombia	9.4	0.1	0.6	0.0	8.4	0.2	2000.9	27.0	18.7
Venezuela	0.0	0.6	0.0	0.0	0.3	0.3	71.7	0.3	1.1
Mexico	-2.6	-1.9	0.8	0.2	7.1	0.8	1119.0	11.1	4.5
Bangladesh	0.0	-0.6	0.0	0.0	0.1	0.1	78.9	1.4	-0.4
India	0.1	-3.7	1.2	0.5	8.2	0.3	1054.3	11.3	6.5
Indonesia	-3.9	-1.4	1.5	2.1	16.5	8.5	3008.5	10.7	23.4
Korea (Rep.of)	0.0	0.0	1.1	0.0	1.8	10.6	1490.9	-0.2	13.5
Malaysia	0.0	-1.1	0.0	4.0	13.7	1.9	1990.3	4.7	18.5
Thailand	-0.9	0.0	1.5	0.1	12.7	22.2	3699.3	2.6	35.4
Africa	-49.6	-17.8	-30.4	-10.1	-48.5	-20.7	4005.4	-85.7	-177.1
Latin America	10.8	18.7	18.1	11.6	39.4	13.3	11485.9	92.5	112.0
South Asia	0.2	0.0	2.3	0.6	1.3	0.4	306.8	1.8	4.8
Other Asia	0.1	-9.0	0.8	0.3	11.7	5.5	2441.2	23.0	9.4
ASEAN	0.1	-4.1	4.4	12.4	8.7	15.0	6213.6	38.1	36.5
NIEs Asia	0.0	-3.0	1.7	0.2	46.5	20.7	5869.8	16.1	66.0
Developing countries	-38.4	-15.2	-3.0	15.0	60.2	34.6	30394.6	86.0	53.2
Least developed	-28.1	-1.3	-19.0	-0.9	-8.8	-2.7	1367.6	-25.0	-60.9

(a) as % ACP exports (b) as % other developing country exports (c) as % OECD imports
(d) exclude Bhutan, Kiribati, Myanmar, Samoa

Sources and explanation of price assumptions: see text

In the case of the CBI and CARIBCAN beneficiaries, the erosion of special benefits, i.e. over and above GSP tariff concessions, attached to tropical products in the US and Canadian markets, is much less serious than for the ACP exporters on the EU market. Most tropical products from GSP beneficiaries enter the North American markets tariff-free. The only significant exceptions are a few wood products and crustacea and molluscs, but over all no serious damage is done by simply taking the effects of the erosion of GSP benefits.

The preferential tariff rates and GSP utilisation rates are important in estimating trade shift from the ACP States and the other developing countries in favour of the MFN suppliers. They are also needed for calculating the changes in world prices and the after-tariff prices received by the different exporter groups on different markets. In the case of coffee and cocoa, the price changes were taken from the RUNS model simulation, which gave price reductions of 1.5% for coffee and 1.2% for cocoa. The tariff reductions themselves might be expected to result in price increases, but the reductions are small and only apply to EU imports. As a result the model suggests that interactions among markets, in particular the more substantial liberalisation in temperate products and manufactures, will lead to substitution and income effects, resulting in reductions in demand for tropical beverages. In the case of tobacco, vegetable oils and other tropical products, price effects and trade changes were estimated with the partial equilibrium model.

Table 3.6 shows the effects on export revenues in value terms. Among the ACP states the Côte d'Ivoire and Kenya, and among other developing countries, Colombia and Costa Rica, which have ACP-type privileges because of the Andean and Central American concessions, particularly affected. The EU tariff cuts in their 'non-traditional' exports, vegetables, fruit flowers and plants, are also atypically large.

The calculations show a small overall improvement, whether in volume or value terms, for the developing countries as a whole, though the ACP states suffer negative effects, in revenue terms equivalent to $ 177 million or just over 3% of exports. Trade shift from the ACP benefits the other developing countries and their export earnings improve, except in the case of tobacco where the rise in world prices is not sufficient to offset trade shift in favour of the MFN suppliers. It may also benefit the US. The US expects to expand its horticultural exports to the EU (Kantor, 1994) because of the erosion of preferences. In coffee and cocoa, falls in world market prices lead to deteriorating revenues for the developing countries as a while, though there is still some trade shift towards the non-ACP producers as the tariff preference margin is eliminated.

4. Trade in industrial products

Trade with developed countries

The main MFN tariff reductions that emerge for the Uruguay Round are summarised in Table 4.1. On average MFN tariffs are reduced by 2.4 points. Some of the highest tariff rates have the smallest reductions. The rates on textiles and clothing are larger than average, but remain the highest. This is also the sector where the quantitative limitation of trade through the MFA has become pervasive. The gradual dismantling of the MFA will go further than the tariff cuts to open the markets of the industrialised countries to exports from the developing countries (see Chapter 5). Leather, rubber, footwear and travel goods, and transport equipment all had well above average tariff rates and small cuts, although electric machinery is significantly cut.

The GATT Secretariat has calculated that the reduction in developed country tariffs on industrial goods imported from other developed countries, weighted by their export mix, averages 2.4 points, as against 2.5 points for developing country exports but only 1.7 for exports from the least developed, which (because of the composition of their exports) now face the highest average tariff (GATT, 1994 *Access*). However the Secretariat argues that a more realistic picture is given if textiles and clothing are excluded, because of the off-setting gains from the phasing out of the MFA. When textiles and clothing and fish and fish products are excluded the reductions in tariffs are still 2.4 and 2.5 for developed and developing, but only 1 point for the least developed. This cut for the least developed, however, is from 1.7 to 0.7, still the lowest rate. (No reason is advanced to justify the exclusion of fish.)

For both ACP and CBI countries, tariff preferences on industrial goods (apart from textiles and clothing) do not – cannot – generally go beyond the zero-tariff GSP preferences. Thus in this category we simply estimate the effects of the erosion of GSP benefits. There are a few exceptions where industrial products are excluded from the EC GSP but where the ACP countries continue to enjoy tariff-free access, or from the US and Canadian GSPs where CBI countries have preferential tariff access. In the former case the items, mostly basic minerals and chemicals, have not been excluded from the calculations in Table 4.2, which then will marginally overestimate the losses to the ACP beneficiaries and underestimate the gains to other developing countries.[14]

For the ACP states and for the developing countries as a whole trade shift towards the developed countries because of their loss of preferences results in deteriorating trade balances in industrial goods (see Table 4.2). (Textiles and clothing are excluded.) ACP export earnings are damaged particularly in metals and minerals (which include gold and precious metals and stones), in wood, pulp and paper and in the residual 'other industrial products' group. The Bahamas explain about half of the ACP figure for chemicals, with Trinidad and Tobago accounting for much of the rest. The Dominican Republic and Surinam show negative figures for electrical equipment and other industrial products.

In most categories the rise in the world price more than offsets the volume effect of trade

---

14. For the CBI, the excluded items include some leather goods including footwear, petroleum and petroleum products. In some of these cases, e.g. footwear and the relevant petroleum products (kerosene and motor spirits), CBI countries benefit from reduced tariffs and it is assumed that these rates will not be changed. In others, including petroleum, MFN rates are so small (0.5% in that particular case) that the distortion will be minimal.

42

Table 4.1: MFN tariff reductions offered by the developed countries (excluding petroleum) ($ US billions and %)

Product category	Import value	Average tariff		
		Pre-	Post-	Reduc-tion
All excluding petroleum	736.9	6.3	3.9	2.4
Textiles and clothing	66.4	15.5	12.1	3.4
Metals	69.4	3.7	1.5	1.7
Minerals, precious stones and metals	72.9	2.3	1.1	1.2
Electric machinery	86.0	6.6	3.5	3.1
Leather, rubber, footwear and travel goods	31.7	8.9	7.3	1.6
Wood, pulp, paper and furniture	40.6	3.5	1.1	2.4
Fish and fish products	18.5	6.1	4.5	1.6
Non-electric machinery	118.1	4.8	2.0	2.9
Chemicals and photo. supplies	61.0	6.7	3.9	3.0
Transport equipment	96.3	7.5	5.8	1.7
Manufactured goods nes	76.1	5.5	2.4	3.1

Source: GATT, 1994 *Access* with amendments.

shift and there is an overall positive effect for the developing countries. In electrical equipment and non-electrical machinery trade shift is most serious for the developing countries as a group and these two sectors result in a small negative overall effect on total export revenues. Among individual countries Mexico, Brazil and Korea stand out as particularly affected, as do the NICs as a group.

Trade among developing countries

Up to this point we have concentrated on trade between the developing countries and the industrialised countries. However, the Uruguay Round market access agreement also brought opening of access on the part of the developing countries themselves. This will provide benefits in the form of enhanced exports, with indirect effects on investment and growth, without the negative implications of the loss of preference margins associated with liberalisation by the developed countries. This trade has grown rapidly relative to North-South trade over recent years. During the 1970s the share of developing country imports from other developing countries rose from 19% to 30% though since then it has levelled off (UNCTAD, 1993 *Handbook*). The structure of developing countries' exports for 1970 and for 1990 is given in Table 4.3. The most striking feature is the rise in the importance of South and South East Asia as a destination for developing country exports.

Our estimates of the effects on trade in temperate agricultural goods already take into account agreed commitments of the developing countries to open their markets. Data on the details of the tariff reduction offers of the developing countries are not yet available. Although the major decreases in the former high-tariff countries in Latin America preceded the Round,

Table 4.2: Industrial products, changes in export value, excluding textiles and clothing
(US $m)

	metals minerals	wood paper	leather footwear	chemicals	elec.equip	nonelect. mach.	trnspt equip	other industrial	OECD Imports 1992	shift + creation	change in value
Share in OECD impts, %											
ACP	6.3	1.4	0.4	0.9	0.1	0.0	0.1	0.4			
other developing	38.8	16.1	36.2	11.7	27.0	13.3	5.3	17.1			
MFN countries	54.9	82.4	63.5	87.4	72.9	86.6	94.6	82.5			
Change in:											
world price	1.7	2.3	1.5	2.6	2.9	2.7	1.6	2.3			
EU price	-0.4	-0.6	-0.4	-0.7	-1.3	-1.0	-0.4	-1.0			
Trade shift from											
ACP (a)	-0.9	-2.0	-2.1	-4.0	-4.1	-3.5	-2.3	-3.2			
other developing (b)	-0.0	-0.4	-0.3	-0.3	-1.3	-2.0	-0.5	-0.8			
Trade creation (c)	0.5	0.8	1.0	1.9	1.5	1.6	1.2	1.2			
Angola	-2.6	-0.0	-0.0	-0.0	-0.0	-0.1	-0.1	-0.6	207	-2.3	-3.3
Botswana	-1.4	-0.0	-0.0	0.0	-0.1	-0.3	-0.0	-0.3	119	-1.5	-2.1
Cameroon	-1.1	-8.3	-0.0	-0.0	-0.0	-0.1	-0.0	-0.5	414	-7.7	-10.1
Côte d'Ivoire	-1.5	-8.7	-0.0	-0.0	-0.1	-0.1	-0.0	-0.8	465	-8.6	-11.3
Ethiopia	-0.0	-0.0	-0.0	-0.0	-0.0	-0.2	-0.0	-2.2	59	-1.9	-2.5
Ghana	-4.3	-3.8	-0.0	-0.1	-0.1	-0.1	-0.0	-1.0	492	-6.8	-9.4
Kenya	-0.2	-0.1	-0.0	-0.4	-0.3	-0.3	-0.0	-2.7	107	-3.1	-4.0
Malawi	-0.0	-0.0	-0.0	-0.0	-0.0	-0.1	-0.0	-0.1	6	-0.2	-0.3
Mauritius	-0.4	-0.0	-0.2	-0.0	-0.1	-0.2	-0.0	-3.1	121	-3.1	-4.0
Mozambique	-0.0	-0.0	-0.0	-0.0	-0.0	-0.1	-0.0	-2.9	79	-2.4	-3.1
Nigeria	-0.2	-0.5	-0.0	-0.2	-0.2	-0.5	-0.1	-7.3	232	-6.9	-8.9
Senegal	-0.3	-0.0	-0.1	-0.0	-0.2	-0.2	-0.0	-3.0	112	-3.0	-3.9
Somalia	-0.0	-0.0	-0.0	-0.0	-0.0	-0.0	-0.0	-0.4	9	-0.3	-0.4
Sudan	-0.0	-0.0	-0.0	-0.0	-0.0	-0.1	-0.0	-0.5	18	-0.6	-0.7
Tanzania	-0.5	-0.1	-0.0	-0.0	-0.0	-0.1	-0.0	-0.5	61	-1.0	-1.4
Zambia	-8.1	-0.0	-0.0	-0.0	-0.0	-0.0	-0.0	-0.1	596	-5.6	-8.2
Zimbabwe	-3.9	-0.0	-0.0	-0.0	-0.2	-0.2	-0.0	-1.9	344	-4.5	-6.3
Guyana	-1.5	-0.1	-0.0	-0.1	-0.0	-0.0	-0.0	-0.8	137	-1.9	-2.6
Jamaica	-2.1	-0.1	-0.1	-0.6	-0.2	-0.1	-0.0	-16.3	575	-15.0	-19.5
Fiji	-0.0	-0.7	-0.2	-0.0	-0.1	-0.0	-0.0	-1.0	62	-1.6	-2.0
Papua-New Guinea	-4.6	-4.0	-0.0	-0.0	-0.0	-0.1	-0.0	-0.8	515	-7.0	-9.6
ACP (66)	-86.1	-42.7	-7.2	-39.4	-15.9	-5.5	-12.1	-116.3	12766	-247.8	-325.2
Argentina	1.1	0.5	0.5	1.8	-0.0	-1.5	0.7	1.2	1624	-12.6	4.2
Brazil	50.4	6.6	9.9	9.4	-1.1	-16.7	6.6	4.7	15050	-86.6	69.8
Colombia	3.8	0.2	0.6	0.2	-0.0	-0.2	0.0	0.5	885	-4.0	5.1
Chile	31.4	3.5	0.1	2.5	-0.0	-0.1	0.1	0.5	4196	-7.3	37.9
Mexico	13.0	2.0	2.4	12.1	-24.0	-43.7	36.6	9.6	30648	-312.1	8.0
Venezuela	8.2	0.1	0.0	2.1	-0.0	-0.3	0.4	0.7	1569	-6.3	11.2
Bangladesh	0.0	0.0	0.1	0.0	-0.0	-0.0	0.4	0.4	392	-3.0	-.9
India	35.7	0.2	6.6	4.2	-0.3	-2.7	0.7	2.8	7286	-30.2	47.3
Indonesia	13.2	11.4	9.1	1.5	-1.3	-2.3	0.5	0.6	6738	-31.4	32.7
Korea (Rep.of)	6.2	0.9	33.3	8.5	-24.2	-45.1	14.1	12.3	33179	-330.5	6.0
Malaysia	4.6	13.2	0.5	2.3	-20.7	-20.4	1.0	3.1	16922	-187.0	-16.5
Thailand	17.8	1.1	7.7	1.3	-7.3	-23.9	0.8	5.8	13146	-129.3	3.5
Africa	-1237.8	-50.5	-8.9	-41.0	-30.5	-18.2	-19.6	-219.6	20300	-399.3	-526.1
Latin America	139.2	13.7	15.8	38.5	-26.1	-63.3	47.1	0.8	46450	-335.9	165.6
South Asia	37.8	0.3	9.2	4.3	-0.4	-3.0	1.1	4.3	9207	-42.7	53.7
Other Asia	17.2	3.6	55.8	18.6	-16.7	-22.7	3.0	28.9	44739	-361.4	87.6
ASEAN	44.0	26.8	19.2	5.7	-34.5	-51.9	2.4	16.8	46506	-436.5	28.5
NIEs Asia	32.7	9.0	53.9	27.3	-68.8	-325.2	29.5	49.4	118181	-1381.3	-192.4
Developing Countries	291.4	15.0	94.7	67.1	-152.1	-473.4	81.3	-8.0	329077	-3061.0	-213.0
Least developed (d)	-51.2	-6.2	-0.1	-8.7	-2.0	-1.8	-5.9	-34.7	4277	-86.3	-110.6

(a) as % ACP exports (b) as % other developing country exports (c) as % OECD imports (d) least developed exclude Bhutan, Kiribati, Myanmar, Samoa

Sources: see text

44

Table 4.3: Structure of exports of developing countries by region, 1990 (%)

		Developed countries	Eastern Europe and Former Soviet Union	Developing Countries	of which: America	Africa	South and South-East Asia
All products	1970	71.6	7.1	19.9	6.5	2.8	7.7
	1990	63.1	7.7	27.2	3.9	2.6	16.5
Food	1970	73.8	10.5	15.3	3.7	2.6	5.5
	1990	62.4	11.3	26.0	5.3	3.7	10.9
Agric. raw materials	1970	55.5	15.6	22.0	4.0	1.7	14.0
	1990	85.2	9.6	34.0	4.5	3.2	22.8
Ores and Metals	1970	68.1	6.6	6.7	2.3	0.5	2.9
	1990	74.3	7.3	24.3	4.6	1.6	15.3
Fuels	1970	63.9	1.0	20.7	10.0	1.7	6.7
	1990	59.4	2.3	25.1	3.3	3.2	14.3
Manufacturers	1970		9.1	32.5	8.7	7.3	11.9
	1990		7.7	28.5	3.9	2.2	18.4

Source: UNCTAD, (1993) *Handbook.*

these were 'credited' to them, and their total cuts are estimated to average 27%, above their target of 24%. This is an absolute cut of 3 points (Table 4.4). The largest cuts are in food, fish, textiles and transport equipment.

Despite the increases in intra-developing country trade, the increases in market access are unlikely to increase substantially the effects discussed in the last section. Almost two-thirds of developing country exports go to the developed market economies and it is in those markets where the major improvements in access because of changes in regime (in agriculture and clothing), not simply tariffs, will take place.

However while this might be true of the developing countries in aggregate – and it is particularly true of the African ACP countries with their dependence on the EU market – it is not necessarily the case for each individual country. In Latin America, for example, there may be countries whose export dependence on Brazil, or in Asia, their dependence on the NICs, is such that the extent of trade liberalisation in these markets is critical in assessing the overall effect on that country.

Table 4.5 looks at the sources of the imports of six specific countries and for specific product groups looks at the importance of those markets to individual exporting countries. It gives statistics for the share of imports from other developing countries and for the two major sources. The importance of trade with neighbouring countries is evident in the panels for Brazil and Argentina. This not only applies to food and raw materials but also to manufactures. On the whole, however, the importance to the exporting countries of such bilateral flows is muted. But Brazilian imports of cereals account for 6.6% of Uruguay's total exports and 4.8% of Argentina's exports. Bilateral trade flows are particularly important in fuels, although here there are few UR effects. Nearly one third of Iran's exports go to Brazil; nearly a quarter of Oman's to Korea. A more detailed study at country level would be required to assess the extent to which Uruguay Round required (or inspired) opening significantly improves their trade prospects.

The Asian countries are particularly important as importers from other developing countries.[15] Among these the NICs are prominent as importers of manufactures and significant UR tariff concessions by the developing countries are most likely to occur on those imports. In Page *et al.* (1991) we calculated the implications of a 30% across-the-board reduction in NIC tariffs on manufactured imports.[16] As one third of these imports come from other Asian countries (including each other), the impact is particularly favourable for Asia, and for the NICs themselves and ASEAN in particular.

The tariff cuts were estimated to raise imports by the three countries, Singapore, Taiwan and South Korea, by 1.9% or US$ 2 billion. The countries of South and South-East Asia now import some 25% of their manufactured imports from other developing countries, so of that increase, the developing countries as a whole might benefit by some $ 500 million. While this is a small figure, it could be multiplied by about three – an estimate (based on data for 1990 from UNCTAD, 1993) of the ratio of South-South trade in manufactures to imports of those three countries from the developing world – to give a very broad-brush estimate of the effects of developing country trade liberalisation in manufactures. This assumes that the tariff cuts of the three NICs are typical of the developing countries as a whole. Latin American cuts are typically larger, but the share of their trade from other developing countries is typically smaller. In this case the loss of exports to the developed countries through trade shift in favour of other developed countries will be more than offset by new trade generated among the developing countries themselves – in terms of total trade. The numbers are still small but the overall change in developing country exports turns from a negative to a positive figure. South-South trade in primary products will also be affected but much of the trade is either tariff-free or tariffs are low. Tariff barriers are relatively high in agricultural products, both food and raw materials, but together they account for only some 11.4% of South-South trade. Moreover the required reduction of these barriers is smaller for the developing countries. Hence we have not tried to put a figure on the rise in South-South trade in goods other than manufactures.[17]

---

15. The World Bank has recently estimated that Japan and East Asia will account for about one-third to one-half of the increase in world imports between now and 2000 (quoted in US London embassy newsletter August 1994).

16. Hong Kong was omitted since tariffs there are typically zero.

17. Appendix 1 discusses how the growing trade with Central and Eastern Europe and the former Soviet Union may affect the result.

Table 4.4: Uruguay Round tariff cuts by developing countries

Model Sector	Average Tariffs		
	Old rate	New Rate	Reduction
Non-grain crops, wool and other livestock	18.0	13.9	4.1
Coal, oil, gas & other minerals	11.5	9.5	2.0
Processed food, beverages & other manufactures	18.0	13.3	4.7
Trade and transport services	0	0	0
Utilities, construction, other private govt. services	0	0	0
Forestry products	0.1	0.1	0
Fishing products	35.2	8.1	27.1
Paddy rice, wheat and other grains	17.3	13.4	3.9
Textiles	30.3	20.3	10.0
Clothing	14.6	10.8	3.8
Chemicals, rubber	19.1	13.2	5.9
Primary iron and steel	8.7	6.0	2.7
Primary non-ferrous metals	2.7	2.1	0.6
Fabricated metal products	8.5	6.9	1.6
Transport equipment	27.2	17.3	9.9
Merchandise trade	13.5	9.8	3.7[a]

[a] Equivalent to percentage change in rate of 27.4

Source: GATT data (preliminary draft estimates)

Sensitivity analysis

Partial equilibrium analysis is of course sensitive to the elasticities used. The preferred elasticities are given in Table 4.6.[18] The sensitivity of our results to these assumptions is examined by doubling all the supply elasticities and halving the demand elasticities. This gives a 'worst case scenario' for the developing countries. Trade creation and trade shift are both increased and the demand response in the liberalising countries diminished, as is any increase in world prices. The alternatives are compared in Table 4.7. The loss in export revenue for the ACP states increases by a factor of two for industrial goods, while trade creation gives a good boost to the exports of other developing countries. These calculations show that our results are sensitive to assumptions on elasticities. Unfortunately there is no alternative to making assumptions; more econometric research into estimating and re-estimating supply and demand functions would be of great value. The sensitivity of the RUNS model to elasticity assumptions is discussed in Goldin *et al.*, pp. 103–108.

18. The demand and supply elasticities are drawn from, or, where sufficiently detailed studies were not available, based on a large number of econometric studies. In the case of supply elasticities for industrial goods where detailed studies are not generally available and the results of the analysis of much broader categories had to be used. Little work has been done on estimating elasticities of substitution between different suppliers so the assumptions used were largely impressionistic. However the results are extremely 'robust' with respect to differences in the assumptions concerning the elasticity of substitution.

Table 4.5: Total imports of selected countries from developing countries, and shares in exports of the two most important suppliers, by product (SITC category)

Mexico

	Total $ mill	% share in total expts. of largest DC suppliers			
food	297	Chile	0.6	Guatemala	2.4
meat	38	Nicaragua	6.6	Guatemala	0.6
fish	6	Chile	0.0	Thailand	0.0
cereals	64	Vietnam	1.2	Thailand	0.0
sugar	19	Guatemala	1.3	Ecuador	0.0
tobacco	47	Thailand	0.0	Brazil	0.0
wood	29	Bolivia	2.4	Brazil	0.0
min.fuels	246	Peru	2.0	Net.Ant.	2.5
chemicals	274	Venezuela	0.4	Brazil	0.1
manuf (a)	1037	Brazil	0.7	Venezuela	0.8
manuf (b)	175	Korea S.	0.0	China	0.0
manuf (c)	983	Hong Kong	0.2	China	0.2
clothing	333	Hong Kong	0.1	Zimbabwe	5.3

Brazil

	Total $ mill	% share in total expts of largest DC suppliers			
food	1152	Argentina	6.7	Uruguay	0.9
meat	30	Argentina	0.2	Uruguay	0.4
fish	54	Argentina	0.2	Uruguay	0.6
cereals	733	Argentina	4.8	Uruguay	6.6
sugar	23	Cuba	0.6	Argentina	0.0
tobacco	7	Argentina	0.0	Venezuela	0.0
wood	16	Paraguay	1.9	Bolivia	0.3
min.fuels	4359	Saudi Arabia	3.4	Iran	32.7
chemicals	524	Argentina	1.3	Mexico	0.3
manuf (a)	627	Argentina	1.5	Chile	1.8
manuf (b)	801	Argentina	3.0	Korea Rep	0.1
manuf (c)	181	Argentina	0.3	Mexico	0.1
clothing	26	Uruguay	0.8	Hong Kong	0.0

Argentina

	total $ mill	% share in total expts. of largest DC suppliers			
food	503	Brazil	0.8	Chile	0.8
meat	116	Brazil	0.2	Paraguay	1.6
fish	30	Brazil	0.0	Ecuador	0.2
cereals	14	Brazil	0.0	Chile	0.1
sugar	17	Brazil	0.0	Chile	0.0
tobacco	5	Brazil	0.0	Paraguay	0.1
wood	52	Bolivia	2.4	Chile	0.1
min.fuels	295	Bolivia	17.0	Peru	1.6
chemicals	575	Brazil	0.1	Mexico	0.4
manuf (a)	1315	Brazil	2.3	Uruguay	3.5
manuf (b)	2717	Brazil	4.2	Korea Rep	0.5
manuf (c)	790	Brazil	0.0	Paraguay	0.1
clothing	222	Brazil	0.1	Uruguay	2.0

Korea

	total $ mill	% share in total expts. of largest DC suppliers			
food	1821	China	1.0	Thailand	0.9
meat	14	China	0.0	Vietnam	0.2
fish	146	China	0.0	Thailand	0.0
cereals	726	China	0.8	Turkey	0.4
sugar	225	Thailand	0.6	Indonesia	0.0
tobacco	16	China	0.0	Turkey	0.0
wood	723	Malaysia	1.2	Chile	0.6
min.fuels	12169	Saudi Arabia	7.6	Oman	23.9
chemicals	862	China	0.3	Singapore	0.1
manuf (a)	3920	China	1.5	Indonesia	1.6
manuf (b)	3506	Singapore	1.9	Hong Kong	0.5
manuf (c)	660	China	0.3	Hong Kong	0.1
clothing	136	China	0.1	Indonesia	0.1

Indonesia

	total $ mill	% share in total expts. of largest DC suppliers			
food	832	Thailand	0.9	India	0.6
meat	26	China	0.0	Singapore	0.0
fish	4	Bangladesh	0.1	Singapore	0.0
cereals	300	Thailand	0.3	Saudi Arabia	0.1
sugar	107	Thailand	0.3	India	0.0
tobacco	45	China	0.0	Zimbabwe	0.9
wood	2	Malaysia	0.0	Singapore	0.0
min fuels.	1757	Singapore	1.1	Saudi Arabia	1.4
chemicals	1324	Korea Rep.	0.4	Singapore	0.4
manuf (a)	1985	Korea Rep.	1.2	China	0.2
manuf (b)	184	Singapore	0.1	Korea Rep.	0.1
manuf (c)	326	Korea Rep	0.2	Singapore	0.1
clothing	20	Korea Rep	0.0	Hong Kong	0.0

India

	total $ mill	% share in total expts. of largest DC suppliers			
food	235	Myanmar	0.5	Vietnam	1.0
meat	0	none		none	
fish	0	Singapore	0.0	none	
cereals	1	Kenya	0.0	Nepal	0.1
sugar	0	Nepal	0.1	none	
tobacco	0	Singapore	0.0	Bangladesh	0.0
wood	163	Malaysia	0.3	Myanmar	0.5
min fuels.	3047	UAE	7.7	Saudi Arabia	1.9
chemicals	1283	Saudi Arabia	0.3	Korea Rep	0.2
manuf (a)	643	Kore Rep	0.1	Hong Kong	0.0
manuf (b)	285	Singapore	0.2	Korea Rep	0.1
manuf (c)	68	Singapore	0.0	Hong Kong	0.0
clothing	1	Thailand	0.0	Hong Kong	0.0

(a) Manufs. classified by material
(b) mach. and transport equip.
(c) miscellaneous manufactures

Source: UN, Commodity Trade Statistics, 1993

48

Table 4.6: Elasticities and GSP utilisation rates used in the p.e. analysis

| | Assumptions on elasticities | | | | GSP | |
| | demand | export supply | | | substitution (a) | % util'n (b) |
		ACP	GSP	MFN		
tropical products						
coffee beans	-0.31	0.46	0.65	n.a	-10.00	95
cocoa beans	-0.19	0.80	0.80	n.a	-10.00	95
tobacco	-0.40	0.41	0.41	0.70	-5.00	5
veg. oils	-0.51	0.40	0.40	0.49	-5.00	22
other tropical	-0.58	0.60	0.60	0.60	-3.00	3
fish	-0.58	0.50	1.00	1.00	-3.00	4
industrial goods						
metals, mins.	-1.10	0.27	0.27	0.50	5.00	5
wood, pulp, paper	-1.30	0.50	0.50	0.50	5.00	39
leather, footwear	-2.39	0.50	1.00	1.00	1.00	9
chemicals	-2.53	0.50	1.00	1.00	1.00	4
elect. eqpt.	-1.14	0.50	1.00	1.00	1.00	19
non-elect. mach.	-1.62	0.50	1.00	1.00	1.00	28
transport eqpt.	-3.28	0.50	1.00	1.00	1.00	10
other ind. excl clothing and textiles	-1.30	0.50	1.00	1.00	1.00	15

(a) elasticity of substitution between different sources – ACP, GSP and, where appropriate, MDN suppliers
(b) share of GSP-covered imports receiving GSP preferences from GSP data supplied to UNCTAD. In the case of coffee and cocoa beans, by assumption

Sources:

Langhammer (1983), Bond (1983), Islam and Subramian (1989), Adams and Behrman, USDA (1980), Askari and Cummings (1977), Stern, Francis and Schumacher (1977) and other sources quoted in Page et al (1991) and Davenport (1988)

None of the measurements in this chapter takes account of the remaining NTBs against developing countries (in sectors other than agriculture or clothing and textiles). The Uruguay Round commitment to 'rollback' these was not met, although they may be more easily challenged under dispute procedures. This could reduce the benefit from the tariff reductions, at least in the more heavily controlled sectors, like coal and rubber (table 4.8).

Table 4.7: Sensitivity analysis: effects of alternative elasticities (US $m)

	Tropical goods and fish					Industrial goods				
	Imports 1992	preferred elasts.		alternative elasticities		Imports 1992	preferred elasts.		alternative elasticities	
		Volume change	Value change	Volume change	Value change		Volume change	Value change	Volume change	Value change
ACP (66)	5159.8	-83.2	-176.7	-148.5	-275.0	12766	-247.8	-325.2	-848.1	-994.4
Africa	4005.4	-85.7	-177.1	-153.0	-275.6	20300	-399.3	-526.1	-1394.9	-1630.0
Latin America	11485.9	92.5	112.0	165.1	174.3	46450	-336.0	166.0	644.1	830.4
South Asia	306.8	1.8	4.8	3.3	7.5	9207	-42.7	53.7	88.2	129.1
Other Asia	2441.2	23.0	9.4	41.1	14.7	44739	-361.4	87.6	743.6	892.2
ASEAN	6213.6	38.1	36.5	68.0	56.8	46506	-436.5	28.5	776.6	904.0
NICs Asia	5869.8	16.1	66.0	28.7	102.8	118181	-1381.3	-192.4	2728.1	3047.9
Developing countries	30394.6	86.0	53.2	-227.5	-463.2	329077	-3061.0	-213.0	4061.5	4789.3
Least Dvlpd (a)	1367.6	-25.0	-60.9	-56.6	-105.1	4277	-86.3	-110.6	-255.3	-310.8

(a) excluding Bhutan, Kiribati, Myanmar, Samoa

Table 4.8: Sectors which remain affected by post-Uruguay Round nontariff measures.

Product Group (SITC)	Coverage Ratio (%) Quantitative Restrictions
Crude Fertilizers and Minerals (27)	5.0
Metalliferous Ore and Scrap (28)	5.1
Crude Materials, nes (29)	4.9
Coal and Coke (32)	81.3
Chemical Elements and Compounds (51)	4.1
Mineral Tars and Crude Compounds (52)	5.0
Dying and Tanning Material (53)	2.2
Medicinal & Pharmaceutical Products (54)	2.5
Manufactured Fertilizers (56)	5.6
Plastic Materials (58)	7.6
Chemicals, nes (59)	9.6
Leather and Manufactures (61)	5.6
Rubber Manufactures (62)	10.3
Wood Manufactures (63)	0.8
Paper and Manufactures (64)	3.6
Non-Metallic Mineral Manufactures (66)	0.7
Iron and Steel (67)	2.1
Metal Manufactures (69)	0.7
Non-Electrical Machinery	3.4
Electrical Machinery	1.6
Transport Equipment (73)	2.1
Sanitary Fixtures (81)	0.5
Travel Goods (83)	0.2
Footwear (85)	4.3
Scientific Instruments (86)	1.7
Miscellaneous Manufactures (89)	0.8

Source: Yeats 1994

5. Textiles and clothing

The Multi-Fibre Arrangement (with four agreements, so the current version is MFA IV) has regulated imports of textiles and clothing by industrial countries from developing countries since 1974 (and other multilateral agreements had existed since 1962). The current agreement dates from August 1986 and should have expired in 1991, but it was repeatedly renewed to extend it to the settlement and implementation of the Uruguay Round, and is now due to expire at end-1994. It has been a 'permitted derogation' from GATT rules: it is discriminatory; it embodies less favourable treatment for developing countries than developed; it permits unilateral changes (including increases in controls); and it operates through quotas, not tariffs. It is in form a framework for bilateral quota arrangements. These are set by the importers and are administered and operated at the discretion of the exporters, in most major developing country producers: through government allocation. Since the second MFA (1977) importers have had discretion to impose new quotas or reduce existing ones if new products took sales from domestic producers or if there was a rapid expansion within an existing (under-used) quota. For some trade flows (notably those from countries like the ACP who are formally exempt from MFA), parallel measures have been taken, such as 'voluntary' export restraints or surveillance. This is also a sector in which MFN tariffs are among the highest (Table 2.1), and which is frequently excluded from GSP.

During the UR negotiations, the major clothing exporters acted as a bloc, under the International Textiles and Clothing Bureau, to secure the ending of the MFA system, with a transitional period. In looking at the length of the transitional period from the point of view of developing countries, it is important to be aware of the nature of the clothing industry in different countries. Some countries, notably China and India, have clear advantages of low labour costs, large supplies of labour, experience and appropriate institutions for marketing and good transport arrangements to the market countries. There are a few potential additions to this list, including Vietnam and Indonesia. These are (or will be) tightly constrained by quotas and could expand substantially, without supply or competitiveness limits, in response to a removal of quotas, even at present tariffs. Other countries have become major exporters at least in part because of the quota restraints on the initial producers. In some cases this was on the base of a large domestic industry which then turned to export. These are mainly among the larger countries, for example Colombia in the 1970s and Thailand in the late 1970s and early 1980s. As they developed and labour costs became less favourable, their exports have declined, but the industry has remained important because of its local base. Hong Kong has ceased to be a major supplier itself, but remains an important participant in the industry as it subcontracts to other suppliers (not only China, but many of the other new suppliers in Africa and the Caribbean as well as Asia), and is a supplier of some non-quota high quality specialised products for which its costs are not a constraint. (In July 1994, the US introduced new rules of origin, to apply from July 1996, to obstruct Hong Kong's use of China as an outward processor to meet its own unused quotas on more basic goods where China has exhausted its own quotas.)

In other countries among the present exporters, although low labour costs were a necessary condition for success, their (initial) freedom from quota was the principal impulse to export, and the industry was directed (and in many cases the textile inputs were supplied) from abroad. Because these were in fact, if not in form, subsidiary factories of the principal producers or the importers (foreign investment is much less important in this industry than supply, design and marketing relationships), their development into major export industries, and then into being subject to quotas of their own, could be extremely rapid. In most cases, they also saw their own costs rise and alternative uses of labour become important so that, like the larger countries, countries of this type have moved or will move out of the sector. This whole process typically can take under 10 years. Until now, the industry has then moved on to the next generation of low labour-cost countries, with absence of quotas often as an additional incentive.

For this reason, given a transition period which allows existing exporters to exit in the normal way, there could be a general agreement among most exporters to accept the form of settlement that was obtained. The apparent heavy losses of exports to some of the less competitive present exporters are no more than they might have expected without a change in the system. The gains to the traditional, most competitive producers, however, will be real as they, rather than the next generation, take share from those who cease to export. There are potential losses to those who might have been the next generation of subcontractors, if they would have become exporters only because they are quota-free, but computing possible losses to potential third party gainers from protection on more efficient suppliers seems as difficult to justify as it would be to perform. In the actual negotiations, under the system of negotiating between principal suppliers and importers, not-yet-suppliers did not have a voice.

On the side of the industrial countries, again the structure of the industry makes the ending of the MFA less significant for individual companies than aggregate figures might suggest. They will still be protected by high tariffs (the averages in Table 4.1 show little reduction, and they include numbers over 30% for the most sensitive products in the US).[19] They may also use other means of protection. A proposal during the negotiations to exclude MFA products from anti-dumping actions was not adopted. There are even signs that (as in food products) safety requirements may be used as deterrents.[20] But industry pressure to protect may also be less than expected. Many of the producing companies are also importers, and the restructuring of the industry has made the textile industry, if not yet clothing, competitive. The growing administrative complexity of the MFA system is becoming a burden. The US clothing industry remained strongly opposed to liberalisation, but for the EU the principal sticking point was reciprocity, particularly opening the largest Asian markets.

The agreement made embodies these varied interests. Under the Uruguay settlement, the basic framework of MFA IV is extended for 10 years. From 1 January 1995 (assuming that ratification occurs in time), importing countries must remove products with a share of at least 16% from their MFA lists and the remaining quotas will have their permitted annual growth rates increased by 16%. (This is another example of GATT's use of percentages on percentages: a permitted growth of 1% becomes 1.16%, while one of 6% becomes 7%; the most restricted continue to have the lowest growth rates.) Each importer must include at least one product from each of the four sectors: yarns, fabrics, clothing and other textile products. After 3 years, on 1 January 1998, the process is repeated, for 17% of products and an additional 25% on growth rates (1.16 goes to 1.45%); on 1 January 2002, a further 18% of

---

19. There will not be an increase in tariffs to offer an alternative to quotas as there is in agriculture.

20. The *Financial Times* (17 August, 1994) reported that the US was restricting inflammable skirts from India, which followed an earlier unsuccessful, attempt to restrict them as not meeting 'folklore' product conditions. On the other hand, rayon skirts with elastic waistbands would seem to require an equally elastic interpretation of 'traditional Indian'.

products and 27% on growth rates; and finally removal of all quotas on 1 January 2005. This means that almost 50% of products remain controlled for the full 10 years. It will be possible to add products to the list (but not to put back those removed during earlier stages). Small suppliers are entitled to one-stage earlier benefits.[21] Benefits to these countries are also relatively small. Since December 1993 when the agreement was adopted, the imposition of new controls, especially against China and India, has continued. There is an additional provision requiring countries to take steps to 'achieve improved access to markets for textile and clothing products through such measures as tariff reductions and bindings, reduction or elimination of non-tariff barriers, and facilitation of customs, administrative and licensing formalities' (Article 7).

The US committed itself politically (during the effort to secure NAFTA ratification) to postponing the phase-out as long as possible, and formally to publishing a schedule of all the reductions from the beginning. The EU plans to give details only at the time of each of the reductions (the first stage was announced on 1 October 1994). Austria, Finland and Sweden will come under the EU scheme when they join the EU; this will increase their restrictiveness. Canada is the only other present importer with quotas and is likely to follow the US scheme. Switzerland and Japan no longer have quotas. Japan, however, established a framework for imposing restrictions in November 1994, and there is industry pressure for controls, especially on Chinese yarns and textiles.

The requirement to include one good from each range at each stage is of little use for a sector with as many product divisions as this one. It will be possible to continue protecting whichever sector is most sensitive to imports (normally clothing) until 2005. Some of the specifications may be at individual product level, although the bulk are likely to be at a slightly more aggregated (10- or 6-digits, respectively, in terms of the trade classification system). For many products, quota utilisation is low, but (especially now because of the long period since the full revision of the MFA) they have never been removed from the list. The exporters, the importers, and GATT studies all suggest that there are enough of these to make the first two stages, 1995 and 1998, ineffectual. Some new suppliers have high permitted quota growth rates and these would gain a little. India has 7% in many products, but even this only becomes 8.2% with a 16% rise. The acceptance of the phasing out of controls on the part of some EU producers was reflected in the willingness of some countries to reduce barriers in the first stage, although pressure by other producers prevented this. The fact that the lists for future stages will be announced at the time means that if this willingness acquires more support the second and third phases could be made more significant. Initial calculations of the effects of proposals for the first stage suggest no immediate effect, and probably no effect from the second stage, so that the effects will come through at the earliest from 2005. (The timing of effects is discussed in Chapter 6.)

Article 7 on access was directed especially at India and Pakistan. The Latin American and ASEAN countries had reduced their tariffs, which had been high in this sector. 'Achieve' was substituted for the first draft's 'promote'. The use of a target (achieving) rather than specifying removal of a barrier, or following a procedure, is unusual in GATT settlements (it

---

21. For the EU, Peru and Sri Lanka; for the US, Argentina, Costa Rica, Jamaica, Macau, Peru and Uruguay (UNCTAD, 1994 *Supplement*, p. 125).

is more like the US interventions to open the Japanese markets to its exports). It could, now that it is included in the settlement, be taken to Dispute Procedure. Although it is difficult to see how much access would be considered to meet the requirement, total absence of imports, as at present, would be actionable. There will also be a Textiles Monitoring Body to review disagreements under the phasing out. Its recommendations will not be binding; if they are not accepted, a dispute can then go to the usual Disputes Procedure.

In attempting to quantify the effects of removing the quotas (for the moment only considering the final effect, not the stages), there are two questions to be asked. What will be the increase in imports by the industrial countries once the quantitative controls are removed (the addition to any normal annual increase)? Will the composition of suppliers among the developing countries change? (No explicit allowance for greater exports to other developing countries is included here because the potential effect of tariff reductions in these was discussed in Chapter 4. There is in principle a possibility that, as long as the MFA survives, the developing country members could impose restrictions on each other, in particular on China which all now fear as the most competitive, but at the end of the phasing out these would also have to go.) Any increase would be principally in the form of a one-off adjustment, a reversal of the net diversion away from developing countries during the period of control. There might, however, also be some long term effect, i.e. a permanently more rapid growth rate, if greater certainty and ease of access, in the absence of the risk of unilateral imposition of new controls and of the burden of quota administration, encouraged increased investment for export in the developing countries.

There is strong evidence that in the past imports from developing countries of products not covered by binding quotas increased significantly more rapidly than those that were (e.g. Erzan *et al.* 1990, p. 76 which found differences between 5.4% and 6.7% for the EC and 2.4% and 13.6% for the US between 1981 and 1987). If the goods controlled by quota are, as might be expected, precisely those which would have grown most rapidly in the absence of quotas, these might be minimum estimates of the additional exports to be expected. Against this the extent of substitution among products and countries suggests that such estimates would exaggerate the opportunities. There was also diversion to suppliers within the EC, especially in the second half of the 1980s, with the accession of Spain, Portugal, and Greece.

Past estimates of the effect of removing the MFA assumed lower increases for textiles than for clothing (cf. Silberston 1989 pp. 87-8). The continuing increase in the competitiveness of industrial countries' textiles industries now makes even these lower increases doubtful. But in clothing, the very high differences in growth rates and the still-strong lobbying against any concessions in the US both suggest that there is some increase in imports to be expected here, and the US accounted for 38% of developing country exports of clothing to industrial countries in 1992 (the EU for 40%; Japan for only 13%). Assuming a substantial increase in US imports from controlled countries of clothing and other finished products, but little growth for the other importing industrial countries or for other textile products, suggests a basic assumption of a rise of about 20% in the level for finished products, equivalent to an increase in the annual rate of rise of 2 points over 10 years). If the increase is in fact general across all industrial countries, this gives a rise of 60% for all OECD countries, or about an extra 5 points a year. The lowest estimate would be of no change.

Table 5.1 shows which countries are important suppliers to the OECD and for which clothing and other textiles are important exports. The last two columns apply the 2% and 5% assumptions to estimate the total change and the effect if all countries gain equally. This is clearly unlikely.

Some countries are very minor suppliers, not at present in any quota scheme, who would gain little or nothing from freeing the market. Others, we suggested, would be moving out of this sector. The current assessment of most exporters, supported by evidence on quota utilisation (and continuing pressure to increase restrictions on them) suggests that India and China are most likely to gain.[22] Pakistan also has the required conditions, especially low labour costs; Korea, with high productivity and access to its own (especially synthetic) fabrics, could do well. The eastern European countries will gain from the preferential phasing out of MFA quotas on them at twice the rate required by the MFA settlement and have the training and technology advantages discussed in Chapter 4. Even if in the longer run this area moves out of the low labour-cost class, it will probably retain some advantage at least for the 10 years, and it would retain exceptional advantages in low transport costs and short delivery times, as well as preferential tariff rates.

Finally, there are those which have gained increases in their exports artificially because they have been not been quota-bound, and have been assisted by those which are. As most countries start with some clothing industry, and many countries with clothing have turned to exporting in the last decade, choosing those which may lose is slightly arbitrary. Identifying those which have achieved very rapid increases to become significant suppliers within less than a decade without apparent special competitiveness advantages and judgements from some of the exporters themselves have been used to draw up the list used in Table 5.2.

Here, the assumption of variants 1 and 2 is that there is no overall increase in OECD imports because of the ending of the MFA, but that there is a concentration of the supplying industry in the most competitive countries, and away from the new marginal suppliers. If these lose 50% of their exports (which would in most cases still leave them above their levels of a decade ago), and if this loss is divided proportionately among the five areas considered to have better than average opportunities, the results are as shown here as variant 1. (The base forecasts are from Table 5.1.) The second variant uses the more extreme assumption that only India, China, and Korea gain. (A still more extreme version would be to concentrate the whole gain in China.) The changes can be combined to give a rough indication of the effect of some overall growth with redistribution. 5% extra annual growth would be sufficient to balance the assumed reductions in share; 2% (shown as variant 3 in Table 5.2) would compensate for slightly under half. Mauritius, Bangladesh, Sri Lanka and the Maldives would still have large falls. Chinese exports of clothing to the OECD countries are still a sufficiently small share of its own total, although large relative to the OECD markets, for the increase to appear modest relative to its total exports. All changes are expressed as percentages of total exports in 1992.

22. This assumes that China joins the WTO and that any transitory requirements do not further restrict its exports. It also assumes that its exports will not meet domestic constraints from rising consumption or supply constraints, e.g. on its output of cotton. On the other hand, it could gain more than calculated here as its exports to other developing countries, mainly in Asia, but also in Latin America. could rise. The total rise in its clothing exports, even under the higher variants, is less than observed for many of the countries which saw their booms in the 1970s and 1980s.

Table 5.1: Exports of textiles and clothing, 1992 [a] (%)

Country	Share in country's exports to OECD countries		Share in country's total exports		Share of country in total OECD imports		Effect on total exports, if finished exports [b] rise, for all countries	
	Clothing	All textile products	Clothing	All textile products	Clothing	All textile products	at 2%	at 5%
Capo Verde	1.66	1.75	1.04	1.09	0.00	0.00	0.24	0.69
Sierra Leone	0.09	0.11	0.09	0.11	0.00	0.00	0.05	0.14
Ivory Coast	0.29	3.19	0.21	2.25	0.01	0.04	0.06	0.17
Burundi	0.34	0.40	0.24	0.28	0.00	0.00	0.06	0.16
Ethiopia	1.87	2.04	1.12	1.22	0.00	0.00	0.25	0.71
Uganda	0.26	6.85	0.25	6.52	0.00	0.00	0.05	0.15
Kenya	3.04	5.28	1.84	3.20	0.02	0.02	0.43	1.24
Tanzania	2.17	20.03	1.33	12.30	0.01	0.03	0.34	0.99
Zambia	0.37	2.37	0.21	1.31	0.00	0.00	0.05	0.13
Zimbabwe	4.43	10.69	2.44	5.88	0.03	0.05	0.56	1.60
Malawi	1.75	5.54	1.53	4.82	0.01	0.01	0.33	0.96
Mozambique	0.97	16.88	0.47	8.14	0.00	0.01	0.10	0.30
Comoros I.	0.60	0.79	0.60	0.79	0.00	0.00	0.13	0.38
Madagascar	5.97	11.18	5.28	9.88	0.02	0.02	1.21	3.48
Mauritius	56.46	58.11	56.46	58.11	0.64	0.38	12.88	36.99
Lesotho	54.99	55.12	4.12	4.13	0.02	0.01	0.90	2.59
Swaziland	0.79	2.25	0.27	0.77	0.00	0.00	0.08	0.22
South Africa	1.37	4.35	0.61	1.95	0.13	0.24	0.14	0.40
Mexico	2.66	3.86	2.66	3.86	1.02	0.85	0.70	2.02
Cuba	0.26	0.55	0.14	0.30	0.00	0.00	0.04	0.12
Haiti	47.70	54.07	47.70	54.07	0.06	0.04	11.71	33.63
Jamaica	30.27	30.55	27.38	27.64	0.33	0.19	6.01	17.26
Belize	14.42	14.51	14.20	14.29	0.02	0.01	3.12	8.95
Bermuda	0.01	0.02	0.01	0.02	0.00	0.00	0.02	0.05
Barbados	7.86	9.17	3.03	3.54	0.01	0.00	0.71	2.04
Antigua	3.99	9.55	1.57	3.75	0.00	0.00	0.47	1.34
Dominica	1.13	1.39	0.75	0.92	0.00	0.00	0.18	0.53
St Lucia	17.24	18.04	17.24	18.04	0.02	0.01	4.32	12.41
Grenada	4.99	5.67	1.96	2.23	0.00	0.00	0.49	1.40
St Vincent	3.15	3.27	2.52	2.61	0.00	0.00	0.55	1.59
Costa Rica	25.75	26.74	27.75	26.74	0.54	0.32	5.95	17.09
Colombia	6.05	7.86	4.77	6.20	0.31	0.23	1.12	3.21
Venezuela	0.11	0.23	0.08	0.16	0.01	0.01	0.02	0.05
Guyana	1.65	1.67	1.46	1.48	0.00	0.00	0.32	0.92
Brazil	1.23	4.10	0.83	2.77	0.27	0.51	0.28	0.80
Chile	0.55	0.98	0.38	0.69	0.03	0.03	0.08	0.24
Nepal	28.40	90.57	28.25	90.08	0.08	0.15	6.20	17.81
Pakistan	23.25	70.35	12.84	38.85	0.83	1.44	4.17	11.98
Bangladesh	70.78	80.50	64.69	73.56	1.30	0.85	14.76	42.39
India	19.81	34.83	12.97	22.82	2.38	2.41	3.25	9.32
Sri Lanka	55.55	59.53	44.87	48.08	1.02	0.63	10.12	29.05
Maldives	67.88	68.16	54.55	54.77	0.04	0.02	11.95	34.31
Laos	69.11	69.47	38.83	39.03	0.03	0.02	8.51	24.45
Kampuchea	78.28	78.96	78.28	78.96	0.03	0.02	17.15	49.24
Singapore	4.33	4.59	1.70	1.81	0.96	0.58	0.38	1.08
Taiwan	6.31	9.32	4.40	5.97	3.09	2.63	0.96	2.75
China	22.23	32.30	7.74	11.25	5.91	4.85	1.70	4.87
Papua New G.	0.20	0.27	0.10	0.14	0.00	0.00	0.02	0.07
Vanuatu	0.23	0.24	0.18	0.19	0.00	0.00	0.04	0.11
Solomon. I.	1.10	1.17	0.72	0.76	0.00	0.00	0.17	0.48
Fiji	24.47	24.72	16.99	17.17	0.07	0.04	3.75	10.76
Western Samoa	0.74	1.19	0.65	1.03	0.00	0.00	0.14	0.41
Tonga	2.80	4.19	2.52	3.76	0.00	0.00	0.55	1.58
Thailand	10.46	13.98	6.80	9.08	1.96	1.51	1.59	4.58
Malaysia	6.20	7.53	3.15	3.83	1.14	0.80	0.70	2.02
Indonesia	11.12	15.28	7.34	10.08	2.20	1.74	1.67	4.78
Philippines	21.47	23.04	17.58	18.87	1.60	0.99	3.97	11.40
Korea	11.98	16.79	6.94	9.73	4.60	3.71	1.59	4.56

Table 5.1 Continued								
Africa	6.10	8.05	5.15	6.80	4.13	3.14	1.15	3.29
Northern	11.52	13.37	14.05	16.31	3.24	2.17	3.12	8.97
Sub-Saharan	2.26	4.26	1.57	2.96	0.89	0.97	0.35	1.00
Asia	15.42	20.04	8.82	11.46	44.81	33.53	2.06	5.91
South Asia	28.73	48.13	19.16	32.09	5.53	5.33	4.82	13.84
ASEAN	9.55	12.10	6.52	9.26	6.91	5.04	1.49	4.27
NICs	12.96	15.92	5.97	7.33	17.22	12.17	1.35	3.87
Other Asia	22.89	28.84	17.85	22.50	15.14	10.98	4.24	12.17
Latin America	4.49	6.18	3.68	5.07	4.88	3.86	0.87	2.50
Middle East	1.56	2.97	0.89	1.70	1.14	1.25	0.21	0.61
Eastern European	9.05	12.43	4.26	5.85	3.51	2.78	1.00	2.88
Total non-OECD excluding E. Europe	10.03	13.29	6.34	8.39	56.98	43.42	1.47	4.23
Total Non-OECD	9.97	13.23	6.16	8.18	60.49	46.20	1.43	4.12

Source: OECD, Trade data bank

[a] 'All textile' products includes fibres, yarns, clothing, and other textiles
[b] 'finished' produces includes clothing and other textiles

Countries with a maximum effect < 0.1% of exports are not listed but are included in totals.

For most African countries, clothing and manufactured textiles are not important exports; the high numbers found for non-clothing products in Table 5.1 are exports of raw materials. They will be largely unaffected by the UR. The African countries for which clothing is important are Mauritius, Lesotho (fairly specialised), and, some way behind, Zimbabwe and Madagascar. Zimbabwe is an example of a country with its own industry, making its initial entry into the market; it is unlikely to be greatly helped by the settlement, but should maintain its position. Mauritius is a clear example of a quota-based industriy in timing, in the initiating role of Asian investment, followed by sub-contracting, and in its complete lack of any domestic base. It is therefore included here among the 'losers'. Clothing is at present a sufficiently high share of Mauritius' exports for a fall in it to suggest major losses. But it has had a history of moving from one export to another to meet new policy conditions. By 1992 it was already below quota on many products (and investing in outward processing in Madagascar) so that it is very possible that its clothing exports would have fallen sharply in the absence of any change in the MFA. Madagascar is a subsidiary of Mauritius, but could maintain a minor place. Sub-Saharan Africa as a whole would gain little from a general increase (even with the higher assumption, only 1% in total), and lose little from a fall in Mauritius' exports. It is still basically outside trade in this sector.

Latin America and the Caribbean have many more countries where clothing is an important export, and therefore which could gain or lose significantly. Especially among the Caribbean countries, many have preferential access to the US through its special schemes for outward processing as well as ACP preferences into the EU, a special arrangement with Canada, and GSP. Haiti has a continuing advantage of extremely low costs, but Jamaica, Costa Rica and Colombia could lose share. But, like Mauritius, they would probably have lost share in the 1990s through the normal process of rising labour costs and spreading quotas, so it is unclear

58

Table 5.2: Variant scenarios if trade in clothing becomes more concentrated (changes as % 1992 exports)

	Base 2%	Base 5%	Variant 1	Variant 2	Variant 3
Countries assumed to lose half their exports					
Mauritius	12.88	36.99	-29.41	-29.41	-16.5
Jamaica	6.01	17.36	-13.73	-13.73	-7.6
Costa Rica	5.95	17.09	-13.29	-13.29	-6.6
Colombia	1.12	3.21	-2.56	-2.56	-1.5
Nepal	6.20	17.81	-14.16	-14.16	-8.0
Bangladesh	14.76	42.39	-33.70	-33.70	-18.9
Sri Lanka	10.12	29.05	-23.09	-23.09	-13.0
Maldives	11.95	34.31	-27.28	-27.28	-15.3
Thailand	1.59	4.58	-3.64	-3.64	-2.0
Indonesia	1.67	4.78	-3.80	-3.80	-2.1
Philppines	3.97	11.40	-90.6	-9.06	-5.1
Effects of the falls on exports					
Sub-Saharan africa			-0.56	-0.56	
Africa			-0.40	-0.40	
Latin America			-0.45	-0.45	
South Asia			-4.17	-4.17	
ASEAN			-2.84	-2.84	
Asia			-0.84	-0.84	
Non-OECD developing			-0.58	-0.58	
Principal exporters					
Pakistan	4.17	11.48			
India	3.25	9.32			
China	1.70	4.87			
Korea	1.59	4.56			
E.Europe	1.00	2.88			
Net effect on exports by					
Africa	1.15	3.29	-0.40	-0.40	0.8
Northern	3.12	8.97	0	0	3.1
Sub-Saharan	0.35	1.00	-0.56	-0.56	-0.2
Asia	2.06	5.91	-0.03	0.18	2.0
South Asia	4.82	13.84	-0.32	3.03	4.5
ASEAN	1.49	4.27	-2.84	-2.84	-1.3
NICs	1.35	3.87	0.47	0	1.8
Other Asia	4.24	12.17	1.90	3.61	6.1
Latin America	0.87	2.50	-0.45	-0.45	0.4
Non-OECD developing	1.47	4.23	-0.12	0	1.4

Variant 1. Total OECD imports from non-OECD countries not listed here unchanged: all 5 princpal exporters rise and countries listed in top panel fall.

Variant 2. As in 1, but only 3 principal exporters rise.

Variant 3. Variant 1 combined with 2% growth for all exports.

Source: calculated using OECD database

how much of the loss in Table 5.2 should be attributed to the MFA phasing out. For Latin America as a whole, the gains or losses from any of these assumptions would be small, although larger for the ACP countries in the area.

The major suppliers and the largest possible changes in distribution are in Asia. Clothing is a principal export for a large proportion of the countries in Table 5.1, including all the South Asian countries, the ASEAN countries, and China. These countries are also (see the fifth and sixth columns of Table 5.1) the main suppliers to the industrial countries. Some are already coming to the end of their economic life as clothing exporters, or will be by 2000: certainly Thailand; probably Indonesia and the Philippines which have had their periods of rapid expansion in the last few years. Others, which have been satellite countries to India and China (and Korea, in terms of dependence on fabric) are considered unlikely to be able to compete with India and especially China, once these are free of quotas. The largest of these losers is Bangladesh. This, however, is misleading. Its exports grew rapidly from 1984 to 1990 because of its (initial) freedom from quotas and low costs, but even under the MFA the erosion since 1990 of both these advantages would have meant lower exports by 2005. It has already started to see a shift to Indonesia and Vietnam, and its dependence on India, China and Korea for marketing and fabric gives it little basis for maintaining the present level of exports in post-MFA conditions. Although its assumed potential loss here may look large, its exports of clothing were negligible a decade ago, so even this leaves it a considerable net rise, and its total exports are only about half of its external revenue (migrant remittances and aid make up the rest). If the OECD market expands, Asia would gain significantly. Any redistribution among suppliers would take place largely within Asia, with the ASEAN countries moving out of the sector, and China and (probably) India gaining.

The prospects for Asian markets themselves to expand rapidly in the next decade are strong, as rising incomes and increasing urbanisation increase the demand for bought and non-traditional style clothing. The reduction of tariffs by the NICs and ASEAN countries and the opening likely to be forced on to India and Pakistan could therefore give important opportunities for the other Asian countries. The Latin American countries have already passed the stages of both liberalisation and urbanisation, and the African are probably not yet (with a few exceptions) there. (They would not be large enough to support a large local industry or to have a comparable effect on their neighbours.) In this sector, as in manufactures (and, as will be seen in Chapter 7, also in services) the largest gains are from the tariff cuts on Asian trade, among themselves and with the industrial countries.

6. Summary of quantifiable effects of the Uruguay Round

Summary of effects on trade

Table 6.1 draws together our estimates of the agricultural and manufactures tariff effects. The overall effect on all developing countries is barely significant. Developing countries as a group are net food importers, the higher world prices will generally mean a higher import bill, but the increase is minimal – $240 million out of a total value of net imports of nearly $18 billion. For certain regions, Africa in particular, and certain countries, Ethiopia, Mozambique, Somalia and Guyana, the deterioration in net trade is much more important. For a number of ACP countries the main damage arises from the loss in the value of exports of beef, sugar or rice which are now sold at well above world prices to the EU under Lomé IV quotas as the internal prices of these are reduced. For other exporters, notably Thailand, Argentina and Brazil, there are important gains.

In the case of tropical products, most developing countries gain from improved access to markets in both the developed and the developing countries. In cases where the EU has maintained tariffs to benefit ACP producers, the ACP producers will lose market share to other producing countries. In other cases, tobacco, oilseeds and oils and fish, MFN tariffs will come down in the developed countries and both the ACP and the GSP countries will experience trade shift. The world market prices, however, will edge up, with the result that overall the developing countries will experience a net gain, albeit of only $53 million in net exports. Again the main losers will be in Africa, with Kenya, Malawi, the Côte d'Ivoire and Zimbabwe particularly affected, and the main gainers in Latin America, including Brazil and Colombia.

In the case of industrial goods, reduced MFN tariffs will lead to some trade shift against the developing world as a whole, as the value of preferences is reduced. However because the utilisation of these schemes has been limited, the MFN cuts do relatively little damage. Africa, because of its deep preferences, and ASEAN countries with high utilisation of GSP are net losers but the other regions gain, so that total loss, again allowing for price changes, is estimated at some $213 million. The net loss in export value is estimated at under half a billion dollars or less than half of 0.1 of a percentage point of net exports. For Africa, for the ACP and the least developed the figures are greater, 1.5, 1.5 and 1.9% respectively, but still modest.

Certain individual countries clearly fare much worse than the regional or other groupings. Ethiopia,[23] Malawi, Mozambique and Guyana lose between 4.6 and 5.9% of total export earnings. No one country gains substantially in terms of total revenues. Thailand is estimated as the greatest gainer but its export revenues are only enhanced by half a percentage point.

Table 6.2 adds the effects calculated in Chapters 3 and 4 to the MFA effects from Chapter 5. The removal of quotas on clothing will increase total exports from developing countries, although the increase may be small because importers have become sophisticated at seeking new sources not bound by quotas. We also expect a substantial change in the sources of clothing exports. The countries which have advantages of labour, skills, and raw materials,

---

23. Since Ethiopia is not a GATT member, it will not necessarily benefit from improved access to non-EU markets. Its net losses could be somewhat greater than calculated in this report.

Table 6.1 Summary of trade effects from agricultural tariff reforms, $ mill. and % of 1992 exports (a)

	change total net exports temperate agriculture	change in value of exports to OECD countries		total change in exports	1992 total exports	change as % of total
		tropical agriculture	industrial products			
Angola	-10.7	-0.5	-3.3	-14	3,698	-0.4
Botswana	-13.1	0.0	-2.1	-15	1,742	-0.9
Cameroon	-3.3	-9.9	-10.1	-23	1,990	-1.2
Côte d'Ivoire	-7.7	-33.1	-11.3	-52	6,220	-0.8
Ethiopia	-3.9	-3.5	-2.5	-10	169	-5.9
Ghana	-5.9	-6.1	-9.4	-21	983	-2.2
Kenya	-3.7	-20.5	-4.0	-28	1,339	-2.1
Malawi	-1.7	-17.9	-0.3	-20	383	-5.3
Mauritius	-28.5	-1.1	-4.0	-34	1,292	-2.7
Mozambique	-3.8	-0.8	-3.1	-8	171	-4.6
Nigeria	-17.4	-5.8	-8.9	-32	11,886	-0.3
Senegal	-7.2	-4.1	-3.9	-15	667	-2.3
Somalia	-1.8	0.0	-0.4	-2	75	-2.9
Sudan	-3.0	-0.2	-0.7	-5	420	-1.2
Tanzania	-2.1	-5.2	-1.4	-9	418	-2.1
Zambia	-0.6	-0.7	-8.2	-10	1,050	-0.9
Zimbabwe	-6.3	-16.0	-6.3	-29	1,500	-1.9
Guyana	-10.4	-0.1	-2.6	-14	291	-4.9
Jamaica	-13.7	-1.2	-19.5	-34	1,051	-3.3
Fiji	-2.7	-1.0	-2.0	-6	735	-0.8
Papua New Guinea	0.9	-7.2	-9.6	-16	1,560	-1.0
ACP (55) (b)	-217.7	-176.7	-325.2	-720	48,166	-1.5
Argentina	94.9	7.0	4.2	106	12,235	0.9
Brazil	29.6	31.9	69.8	131	35,862	0.4
Chile	-6.8	6.7	5.1	5	9,986	0.0
Colombia	0.6	18.7	37.9	57	6,917	0.8
Mexico	-7.0	1.1	8.0	2	27,618	0.0
Venezuela	-16.5	4.5	11.2	-1	14,099	0.0
Bangladesh	-9.3	-0.4	-0.9	-9	2,272	-0.4
India	2.2	6.5	47.3	56	19,563	0.3
Indonesia	-10.4	23.4	32.7	46	33,861	0.1
Korea (Rep. of)	46.9	13.5	6.0	66	76,632	0.1
Malaysia	24.3	18.5	-16.5	26	40,705	0.1
Thailand	130.8	35.4	3.5	170	32,473	0.5
Africa	-219.5	-177.1	-526.1	-923	60,927	-1.5
Latin America	24.2	112.0	165.6	301.8	134,727	0.2
South Asia	-32.0	4.8	53.7	26	28,946	0.1
Other Asia	-211.3(c)	9.4	87.6	-114	538,445	0.0
ASEAN	191.5	36.5	28.5	256	116,862	0.2
NIEs Asian (c)	157.3	66.0	-192.4	18.1	348,487	0.0
Devel. Count's.(c)	-241.3	53.2	-213.0	-401	102,818	-0.0
Least developed (d)	-106.8	-60.9	-110.6	-278	14776	-1.9

(a) Discrepancies between this table and previous tables reflect the 'harmonized' country coverage

(b) the following ACP States were omitted from the calculations owing to lack of data:
Sao Tome and Principe, Seychelles, Antigua and Barbuda, Bahamas, Dominica, St Kitts and Nevis, St Lucia, St. Vincent, Kiribati, Equatorial Guinea, Cape Verde, Djibouti

(c) excludes Taiwan. Other Asia includes Hong Kong, Singapore and Korea (Rep. of)

(d) exclude Bhutan, Cape Verde, Djibouti, Equatorial Guinea, Kiribati, Myanmar, Samoa, Sao Tome e Principe

Source: see text for estimates, 1992 data from *International Financial Statistics* and FAO, SOFA93 data bank

Table 6.2: Summary of trade effects, including MFA reform, % of 1992 exports

	Effect of agriculture and tariffs	Effect of MFA with 2% growth and redistribution	Total
Angola	-0.4	0	-0.4
Botwsana	-0.9	0	-0.9
Cameroon	-1.2	0	-1.2
Cote d'Ivoire	-0.8	0	-0.8
Ethiopia	-5.9	0.3	-5.6
Ghana	-2.2	0	-2.2
Kenya	-2.1	0.4	-1.7
Malawi	-5.3	0.3	-5.0
Mauritius	-2.7	-16.5	-19.2
Mozambique	-4.6	0.1	-4.5
Nigeria	-0.3	0	-0.3
Senegal	-2.3	0	-2.3
Somalia	-2.9	0	-2.9
Sudan	-2.1	0	-1.2
Tanzania	-2.1	0.3	-1.8
Zambia	-0.9	0.1	-0.8
Zimbabwe	-1.9	0.6	-1.3
Guyana	-4.9	0.3	-4.6
Jamaica	-3.3	-7.6	-10.8
Fiji	-0.8	3.8	3.0
Papua New Guinea	-1.0	0	-1.0
ACP	-1.5	-0.2	-1.7
Argentina	0.9	0	0.9
Brazil	0.4	0.3	0.7
Chile	0.0	0.1	0.1
Colombia	0.8	-1.5	-0.7
Mexico	0.0	0.7	0.7
Venezuela	0.0	0	0
Nepal	0	-8.0	-8.0
Bangladesh	-0.4	-18.9	-19.3
India	0.3	7.4	7.7
Indonesia	0.1	-2.1	-2.0
Korea (Rep. of)	0.1	3.6	3.7
Malaysia	0.1	0.7	0.8
Thailand	0.5	1.6	2.1
Taiwan	0	1.0	1.0
China	0	3.9	3.9
Africa	-1.5	0.8	-0.7
Latin America	0.2	0.4	0.6
Asia	0.0	2.0	2.0
South Asia	0.1	4.5	4.6
Other Asia (c)	0.0	6.1	6.1
ASEAN	0.2	-1.3	-1.1
NICs	0	1.8	1.8
Devel. Countries	0.1	1.4	1.3
Least dvlpd	-1.9	-0.2	-2.1

Sources: Tables 5.1, 5.2 and 6.1

but which have been constrained by quotas, will regain their shares. In terms of present shares, this will be from the countries which have gained from being low-cost, unconstrained, substitutes. The long-term change in the industry, however, is probably that the substitute countries will be replaced by the most efficient, giving a more concentrated structure, rather than by a new generation of substitutes. It is these potential substitutes which will lose a potential opportunity.

The conclusion is the same as in our preliminary report (Page, *et al.* 1991), given the change to the more pessimistic assumption about the increase in OECD demand for clothing (Table 6.3).. The total gain for all developing countries is about 1.4% of the value of their exports. If the aggregate effect seems small, it must be remembered that, except in the case of temperate agricultural products where a general equilibrium model is used, it excludes the 'knock-on' effects of export opportunities on investment and technology transfer and associated productivity gains. But if the initial trade effects are small, these dynamic effects are also likely to be small. Even if they were to equal the static trade effects, for most countries the overall effects would still be very limited.

In net terms the gains come largely from clothing, and are therefore concentrated in Asia, notably South Asia and China, with small gains and losses for agricultural goods (tropical and temperate) in Latin America and Africa respectively. These have only small gains on clothing on the assumptions here about the MFA phase-out. The ACP and least developed classifications correspond closely to sub-Saharan Africa, and show a similar pattern.

Almost all the individual sub-Saharan African countries lose (because of the combined effects of losing preference on tropical products and manufactures and facing higher costs for their temperate imports). With most of their exports, and all of those to their dominant market, the EU, already tariff-free, it is difficult to see how they could have gained, especially given the dependence of many on the distortions caused by past protection in agriculture. Latin America has some gains, because the more favoured developing countries in other regions lose in preference and because some of its goods will receive tariff reductions, and it has some scope relative to them for gain on clothing. Agriculture is of little importance to most Asian countries, although Thailand will make useful gains. The ASEAN countries have only a small gain from lower tariffs in their markets (excluding gains to the NICs) and could lose those gains as their membership in GSP is phased out. Although some are major clothing exporters now, they seem unlikely to be those which will gain in the longer run as their costs are higher than the most competitive, and rising. India, Korea and China are the gainers, with China likely to have the additional gain of greater security of access in all markets once it enters the WTO and faces a reduced risk of losing MFN treatment.[24]

Compensating losers

The results suggest that there could be some justification for using the provision in the agreement for food aid or supplementary finance for countries damaged by higher-cost food

24. The US has, however, explicitly reserved and strengthened its right to exclude a new member of the WTO from MFN provisions; other countries could, but are unlikely to, do so. If, however, the US gives China MFN, once it is in the WTO, it probably could no longer withdraw it.

Table 6.3: Comparison to previous forecasts (% of 1992 exports)

| | 1991 | | 1994 |
	Central	Low	
Africa	0.5	-0.3	-0.7
Latin America	1.5	-0.9	0.6
Asia	3.5	1.6	2.0
South	5.5	2.8	4.6
ASEAN	2.1	1.6	-1.1
NICs	2.0	0.8	1.8
Other			6.1
ACP	-1.3	-1.5	-1.7
All developing	2.8	1.3	1.4

Source: Page *et al.* 1991; Table 6.2.

imports, especially as these countries do not gain on the other parts of the agreement. If this uses food aid, it could reduce the gains to food-exporting developing countries, although the quantities are unlikely to be significant. A more serious risk to both equity and the world trading system is setting the precedent of compensating countries for losing an advantage they only gained from a previous distortion when there is a return to more normal trading conditions, and offering such compensation only for one source of loss. On the figures in Table 6.2, it appears that some of the most serious losses are suffered not by food importing countries but by those which may lose share in the clothing trade. This suggests two objections to the committment to giving special protection to the food importers. It was argued in Chapter 5 that some clothing exporters' past and present gains were always likely to be short-term. They should therefore be treated like any gain from a temporary trading advantage: to be exploited, but not treated as a permanent source of income. A similar argument could apply to those countries which benefited from the subsidised imports resulting from food surpluses in the industrial countries.[25]

On the other hand, if the subsidised food importers will now receive compensation, it is difficult to see why other countries in analogous positions should not. Analyses by about 16 African countries, with GATT consultants, suggested a variety of expected losses (UN Economic Commission for Africa, 1994). Of the 13 expecting disadvantages from the Round, 8 cited the increased cost of food, but 9 mentioned erosion of preferences. Although loss of clothing exports is largely an Asian problem, two expected this. Four complained of loss of tariff revenue and five of increased costs from the need to adopt and administer higher

---

25. It could be argued that there is a parallel with Dutch Disease, allowing a finite and short-lived gain from exports of a mineral resource to distort an economy permanently by allowing other more permanent sectors to become uncompetitive.

technical standards or other non-trade aspects of the settlement. The last two could be considered costs which should be borne by the trading system as a whole because they are the costs allied to the benefits from the reforms. Compensating the costs of losing the benefits of past distortions is less defensible. If this principle is accepted as a new trading rule, negotiating any reduction in trade barriers in future will be complicated by adding a third party, with an interest in preventing reform, to the traditional GATT model of negotiations between principal importers and exporters.

Timing

It is important for all countries to take account of how trading advantages will change over time. The combination of the staged structure of some of the Uruguay Round settlements and normal lags in adjustment means that it is essential to analyse the evolution of the UR effects over time to inform policy-makers, as well as economic agents, such as farmers and investors, who have to take a view of whether movements in prices, output and trade flows will continue, stabilise or move into reverse. It is not something on which the models used in this report can shed much light. This is an endemic problem with the p.e. models and the RUNS model has not been designed to answer such questions.

There are reasons to believe that the price and output effects of the Uruguay Round are well under way – even in advance of its formal implementation. Several cases where agricultural reforms and tariff cuts have already been made have been mentioned in Chapter 3. The average volume of subsidised EU agricultural exports in 1991–92 was already down by substantially more than 5%, the target for 1995 in the cases of olive oil, sugar, butteroil, fresh fruit and vegetables and alcohol. It was substantially above only in the cases of wheat, beef, poultrymeat, eggs and tobacco. Indeed by backdating the base year for agriculture to the average of 1986–88, the negotiators have ensured that many of the apparently difficult policy decisions and political issues had already been made. The same is true of industrial tariffs in the case of the many developing countries which reduced them on their own initiative.

The remaining reductions in most agricultural and industrial protection will be phased in steadily over the implementation period, generally six years for the developed countries and ten for the developing.

There will then be lags in the effects. A number of decisions were made, often very late in the negotiating process, to allow for the liberalisation process to be slowed. For example, allowing changes in agricultural tariffs and subsidies to start from the period 1991–92. This has the effect of slowing down the adjustment. Secondly, the year-to-year implementation over the six years of the reductions in the volumes of subsidised exports and expenditures on export subsidies may be interprted with flexibilty, allowing for less than full compliance in one year to be made up in later years. In the case of sugar, for example, the EU Commission could avoid any significant cuts in the intervention price, and the levels of the sugar output quotas until 1999.

These lags are in principle captured by the RUNS model. A simulation was done to phase in the adjustments to agricultural protection according to the schedule laid down in the Final Act. By the tenth year, that is the year when the final adjustments have to be implemented by the developing countries, on average some 85% of the final effects had occurred. Because of the strong interdependences in the RUNS model, there were no particularly obvious leading or lagging sectors.

A very rough estimate of the timing of the effects is given in Table 6.4 Given that most of the temperate agricultural reforms in the developed countries were already in place before the Round came to an end, it is assumed that two thirds of the total effects will come through by the end of 1995. In the case of industrial products, the developing countries have already largely implemented their offers, though the developed country tariff cuts will generally wait for the formal implementation. Two thirds of the effect is assumed to occur by the end of 1995. For both of these, we assume that five sixths of the effects will be realised by the end of 1998, 90% by 2001, with complete adjustment by 2005. The effects on OECD imports of tropical products and manufactures begin later, so that we assume that one third of the effect will be seen by 1995, five ninths by 1998, seven ninths by 2001, again with the full effect at the end of 10 years.

The implementation of the MFA, as discussed in Chapter 5, depends on importing countries' choice of what to liberalise first, but once a quota is removed, the lags are probably negligible. Because most of the off-shore industry is based on what are formally one-off contracts, even if they are normally repeated, and frequently the contracts and contacts of the importers are with an agent who can deal with a range of supplying countries, the response in demand is probably a maximum of 6 months. The producers report that setting up a new factory is a matter of months, even if training a new labour force is required. As the US provided a schedule of liberalisation in 1994, and all importers must offer at least three months notice, the effective response time for both demand and supply is negligible. The combination of the assumptions suggested in Chapter 5 about the amount of slack in the present system and the small liberalisations required in the first three stages means that we assume here that there is no effect in the 1995 and 1998 stages, with one quarter coming through in 2001 and the full effect in 2005.

This gives the pattern of Table 6.4, in which the effects on agriculture, positive for the Latin American and some Asian countries and negative for the African (and ACP), come through before the MFA effects, positive for some Asian and slightly negative for other countries. Latin America thus sees a steady improvement through the adjustment period. South Asia, after an initial loss on temperate agriculture, turns positive as first the tropical products and tariff effects, then those of the MFA come through. In contrast, the ASEAN countries see most of their gain come through quickly, but then, because of the assumption made about Philippines and Indonesian loss of competitiveness, lose out from the MFA reforms. The NICs have roughly balancing gains and losses on agriculture and from their own tariff changes in the early years; the positive effects from the MFA come through at the end. Other Asian countries have a more extreme form of the South Asian pattern of losses then gains. Africa loses consistently, and increasingly, on the agricultural side, both on its imports of temperate products and its exports of tropical, but has partially offsetting gains from the MFA by the end of the period. These are not enjoyed by sub-Saharan Africa or the Caribbean, explaining the steadily deteriorating result for the ACP countries.

These results need to be treated with extreme caution. First, all the assumptions about the final outcomes and the path towards it are, as indicated above and in Chapters 3 to 5, subject

Table 6.4: Trade effects over the implementation period (% 1992 exports)

	1995					1998				
	Temperate	Tropical	Mfr Tariff	MFA	Total	Temperate	Tropical	Mfr Tariff	MFA	Total
Africa	-0.24	-0.10	-0.29	0.00	-0.63	-0.30	-0.16	-0.48	0.00	-0.94
Latin America	0.01	0.03	0.03	0.00	0.07	0.03	0.05	0.06	0.00	0.12
Asia	0.01	0.01	0.01	0.00	0.03	0.01	0.02	-0.01	0.00	0.02
South Asia	-0.07	0.01	0.06	0.00	-0.01	-0.09	0.01	0.10	0.00	0.02
ASEAN	0.11	0.01	0.01	0.00	0.13	0.14	0.02	0.01	0.00	0.17
NICs	0.03	0.01	-0.01	0.00	0.03	0.04	0.01	-0.02	0.00	0.03
other	-0.03	0.01	0.01	0.00	-0.01	-0.03	0.01	0.02	0.00	-0.00
ACP	-0.29	-0.12	-0.23	0.00	-0.63	-0.36	-0.20	-0.38	0.00	-0.94
All developing	-0.02	0.00	0.00	0.00	-0.02	-0.02	0.00	0.00	0.00	-0.02
	2001					2005				
Africa	-0.33	-0.23	-0.67	0.20	-1.03	-0.36	-0.29	-0.87	0.80	-0.72
Latin America	0.01	0.06	0.08	0.10	0.27	0.02	0.08	0.12	0.40	0.62
Asia	0.01	0.02	-0.02	0.50	0.52	0.02	0.02	0.01	2.00	2.05
South Asia	-0.10	0.01	0.14	1.12	1.18	-0.11	0.02	0.19	4.50	4.59
ASEAN	0.15	0.02	0.02	-0.33	-0.13	0.16	0.03	0.02	-1.30	-1.08
NICs	0.04	0.01	-0.02	0.45	0.48	0.04	0.01	0.02	1.80	1.88
other	-0.04	0.02	0.02	1.52	1.52	-0.04	0.02	0.02	6.10	6.10
ACP	-0.40	-0.29	-0.53	-0.05	-1.26	-0.45	-0.37	-0.68	-2.20	-1.70
All developing	-0.02	0.00	-0.01	0.35	0.30	-0.02	0.00	-0.01	1.40	1.37

Source: see text for assumptions

to serious uncertainties. Second, all the changes are extremely small. Even the gains for India and China on the MFA could be blunted if the removal of quotas inspires new types of barrier. Third, these are not the actual changes to be expected over the next 10 years, but the amount by which the GATT settlement will cause a departure from all the changes for other reasons which will occur. Finally, many of the effects attributed here to the GATT settlement could plausibly be explained by other factors, and might therefore have been observed in the absence of the GATT settlement. The estimates also can allow for only one type of benefit, to export revenue, and thence to national income. For the countries which are reducing their own barriers there will be other income effects from lower prices, directly, and through the increased competition for local producers.

Welfare effects

In order to look at welfare or real income effects of the changes discussed so far we revert to the RUNS model simulations. These have the great advantage over p.e. estimates of taking

68

into account the principal dynamic effects on investment and economic growth. As a measure of the UR effects on real income, the RUNS model evaluates a welfare index modified for distorted open economies (Goldin et al., 1993). Although complex in theoretical formulation, the welfare measure has a simple intuitive interpretation as the change for households from the base-run level of utility. What differentiates the measure from the usual real income measures used in general equilibrium models is that it takes specific account of the welfare losses to consumers of tariffs or tariff equivalents, net of actual public finance revenues.

Table 6.5 shows the real income effects at the end of the simulation period, the year 2005, relative to GDP in the base simulation. Like all the RUNS simulations, it excludes MFA effects and the direct effects on the areas' income of their own tariff cuts (and of their opening to services).

In terms of the change in GDP, after all changes have had a chance to work themselves through, the net effects on the developing countries are small, but generally positive, the exceptions being Indonesia, Africa and the Mediterranean. Indonesia exports rice, where the price rise is small, and coffee and cocoa which decline in price. It imports wheat, meat and dairy products whose prices rise. As a result Indonesia's terms of trade decline. Africa is a net importer of all our food categories except sugar. Though the price of sugar rises more than that of most other foods this is far from enough to prevent deterioration in their terms of trade.

Table 6.5: Changes in economic welfare from RUNS Model Simulation (percentages)

	% of base GDP
Africa	-0.3
Latin America	0.2
South Asia	0.4
Other Asia	1.4
Total	0.6

Source: see text

Distribution of benefits

Some results seem firm. The countries which will gain most are those which have been constrained most in the past, by agricultural protection (southern hemisphere producers, including Latin America) or by the MFA (Asian producers, notably China, perhaps in the medium term the eastern European), along with countries entering on the export of those manufactures for which tariffs are coming down (again China). The gain will come through fully for countries which do not have access to preferential schemes (China), and therefore cannot lose from their erosion; partially for those countries with only the minimum, general, level of preferences (most of Latin America and Asia), and hardly at all for the most preferred (sub-Saharan Africa and the Caribbean). The gain will be increased for countries which are also new entrants to GATT/WTO, and which will therefore be gaining from all past opening of markets (China again). Exporters to those NICs which had high tariffs and also to Australia and New Zealand, which had avoided large tariff cuts in previous rounds, may also gain more than the average. This is likely to benefit principally the Asian countries. The ASEAN and NIC countries could lose preferences as the GSP system is phased out for them, but they have already passed the key point of needing an entry into the major markets, and are passing from the high-tariff type of exports (clothing and other light manufactures) into more high-technology goods, normally with lower tariffs.

The countries which still produce principally primary goods and whose few non-traditional primary and manufactured exports have received the most preferential terms necessarily have little to gain and the probability of losses. They not only lose in terms of their present exports, but also lose the potential to use preferences in the future as a way of entering markets and gaining export experience in the early stages of their development. They also lose the chance which some might have had of being temporary 'creatures of the MFA' as the need to search for new quota-free suppliers disappears. Offering them temporary compensation, perhaps with conditions, for only one type of loss does not seem either an adequate or an appropriate answer. What they need is a substitute form of assistance for meeting the obstacles to finding and entering new markets with new goods.

7. Services

The approach to international regulations

One of the US objectives in proposing a new Round of trade negotiations in the 1980s was to open other markets to its exports of services. At the time, most other participants were doubtful or opposed, so that this side of the negotiations was put under a special group and the outcome is distinguished from GATT as the General Agreement on Services (GATS). Growing awareness of the opportunities for trade in this sector, however, greatly increased support for the idea during the negotiations. The developing countries also realised their own advantages, from low labour costs and new, more modern structures in some areas, notably air, shipping and construction. The shift away from policies of government sectoral intervention also meant greater willingness to import sensitive services, for example in finance. Except for minor provisions on the timing of submitting the offers and on their need for information and technical assistance, there are no special provisions for developing countries.

From the beginning, the types of demands made went beyond what is meant by 'access' for goods. This is partly because of the nature of intervention in services. Although there are some taxes and fees which are equivalent to tariffs in trade in goods (port and customs service charges; taxes on travel or transport services, etc.), many more obstacles are either in the form of direct government regulation or limits on setting up a distributor in the foreign market. For this reason, the negotiations quickly went into areas of within-country regulations and rules on investment which go beyond the boundaries, even after this Round, of international regulation of trade in goods. What is not clear, and does not seem to have been considered, is why taxation has been so little used and regulation so extensively. The latter may be because services have certain essential differences from goods (with exceptions on both sides). They are intangible, often tied to a specific time, or contingent on certain conditions (insurance for example). Their quality and reliability are therefore difficult to observe or measure. Regulating the supplier is thus much more important, to both the exporter and the government. They are much more difficult to treat in an arms-length, purely market manner. Restricting regulation may, therefore, change the nature of some of the sectors. The results may be particularly unpredictable if this is done at an early stage in their development, as will happen if developing countries open now under the WTO framework.

The approach of regulating the supplier rather than the service is reflected in the four-way classification of 'means of provision' of services used in the agreed framework: cross-border supply (the direct equivalent of trade in goods); consumption abroad (arguably closely equivalent); commercial presence (effectively taken for granted in trade in goods, but the direct and intangible character of services makes the nature of the presence more critical than the nature of a sales agent for a good); and presence of 'natural persons'[26] (again, a need for this is a consequence of the nature of many services). The last two mean that the services framework implicitly introduces international supervision of rules on both foreign investment and labour mobility.

The ways in which a country's treatment of services can be brought under the WTO are effectively divided into four. The first decision is whether a service will be opened to

---

26. Expatriate workers (companies may be 'legal persons').

international regulation, i.e. incorporated in a country's offer, at all. For those which are, a country can register any of three types of control: restrictions on market access, limitations on national treatment of the supplier, or derogations from the general rule of Most Favoured Nation among suppliers. All of the last three can be at national, sectoral, or individual service level. Most of the offers are subject to some general national restrictions, with additional ones on individual items. For most services and countries, the offers were due in February–March 1994, and where a service is 'offered', the limitations on it must by now be specified. (The least developed countries have an extra year, and amendments to the financial offers are allowed until 1996 because there is a special negotiating group taking this forward.)

It is thus possible to avoid opening a country's service industries and to retain the right to increase current controls, either through not making any offer in some, even most, sectors or by imposing and registering strict restrictions. The registered restrictions can also be specified as unbound, and thus remain subject to unilateral change. But for services which are offered and for which the regulations are registered and bound, the information now found in many of the service offers will remove one of the major *de facto* barriers, lack of an accessible way for exporters to know what the restrictions are. In principle, this is equivalent to the information on tariffs provided to GATT since 1948, but the fact that most or all of the restrictions are based on national legislation, under a variety of headings, means that the gain from having a single source is much greater. The information from the discussions in the Round and now in the 2000 pages of offers may prove the most significant opening, especially on minor services and for developing countries, where the cost of obtaining information would be high. This is to be supplemented by provisions (under the agreement) for information points within countries to interpret the regulations, with 'special priority' (nature unspecified) for the least developed.

The negotiations on services necessarily followed the offer and demand, rather than the formula, mode. Some countries, especially the US, then used the authorisation to register exceptions to MFN to restrict the benefits only to the countries with which agreements had been made, or to those offering reciprocal access.

During the negotiations, the US suggested a special arrangement for financial services, under which a limited number of countries would undertake a common set of reciprocal obligations, and exclude other countries which would not accept the package. This was rejected by the other industrial and the developing countries as too great a departure from normal MFN provisions, but traces of it remain in the final agreement. Financial services are one of the three sectors set for immediate further negotiation (to be completed by 1996). There is an additional 'Understanding on Commitments in Financial Services' as part of the final settlement. Using it is presented as an alternative to making specific commitments at a national level, not a replacement. It constitutes a standard framework of commitments to open countries to foreign banking and insurance services which countries can choose to adopt. Unlike standard service commitments, which are assumed to exclude government, this framework includes public procurement. Combined with the possibility of limiting MFN treatment through specified exemptions, use of this framework could create a weaker form of the special group approach. Many countries, both industrial and developing, have included reciprocity on financial services in their MFN exemption lists, and US national legislation in 1994 introduces this as a requirement. If using this framework approach, reinforced by reciprocity limitations on MFN treatment becomes common, for financial or other services, it may make it more difficult for developing countries either to liberalise gradually or to enter other markets before they have substantially opened their own, as they would have to accept a standard package, rather than liberalise gradually, in order to receive any opening in return. This could be a barrier to entry for new or early suppliers. More generally, the countries not included in any reciprocal network may find themselves relatively disadvantaged because there has been opening to others. In some cases, developing countries, especially among the NICs, were particularly targeted in the negotiations. Where the market countries were not open at all in the past, there is no direct loss and so no right to demand compensation. On the other hand, the loss of potential trade was the justification for making MFN one of the foundations of GATT. Using reciprocity here is a clear derogation from that principle.

Shipping services were also given special treatment. Because of the strong resistance to any settlement by the US, which wanted the sector excluded entirely, all offers are to be considered provisional, again with renewed negotiations to begin immediately.

The listing is on a 'positive list' principle: services not listed in a country's offer are not included. Most of the services offers are now available, and range from pages of detail on which services are open, and with what restrictions, to very restricted offers of limited access to one service. Information for all countries on the destinations, sources, and even value of trade in services is too sparse to estimate which countries will gain from country- and sector-specific opening. As the offers take the form of stating the present (post-UR agreement) regulations for a service, not the change, it is also impossible to know whether or by how much access has been changed, without a detailed study of previous regulations. For many developing countries, there has been opening on a unilateral basis over the last 5–10 years, as in goods, and the offers represent the result of this, rather than a new liberalisation. But the interaction of the domestic policy change, the on-going negotiations, and international pressures from other directions may have increased the liberalisation. In some cases, for example financial services in Mexico, it is possible to see a progression, from a limited liberalisation, by 1991, to a further liberalisation within a regional group (NAFTA), to extension of that liberalisation to all trading partners in the GATT offer. For the industrial countries, the most controversial issues were very publicly negotiated, but were largely between each other, and in some cases the results have been explicitly limited by declared exceptions to MFN treatment.

General characteristics of the offers

The offers on individual sectors were prepared under 11 headings: business, communications, construction, distribution, education, environment, financial, health, tourism, recreation, and transport. Government services (and government procurement) are excluded (unless expressly added, as in the financial framework). Within these, countries effectively used their own classifications and degree of disaggregation, although there exists an international and a specifically GATT sub-classification, with 154 classifications. As formal quantification is impossible, this chapter will look first at developing countries' own offers, to indicate which countries and in what sectors they have made offers and might therefore expect an increase in national income through access to imported suppliers. Then, the three offers of the principal industrial areas will be examined, especially in the sectors expected to be of most interest to developing countries.

The MFN exemptions lists have some common characteristics. Most countries which have bilateral or regional commitments to other countries have included these. Although the equivalent of free trade areas will be permitted under the general agreement, the conditions for this have been strengthened (as they have for goods) to restrict discriminatory groups which are not taken as a step towards full integration or which liberalise only some sectors. Any MFN exemptions registered now, on the other hand, do not need to meet any conditions and cannot be challenged. The formal article of the agreement which deals with such groups refers explicitly to economic integration, going further than the equivalent (Article XXIV) for goods, which mentions customs unions and free trade areas (Hoekman 1993, p. 31). This is partly perhaps an updating, but it also reflects the deeper integration characteristic of trade in services. Some exemptions are for practical reasons, for example where there is a regional transport network, with special provisions among neighbouring countries. These types of restrictions are unlikely to represent changes from the existing situation. Especially in financial services, countries have made reciprocity a condition, either explicitly, or by listing the countries to which they are opening. There are also a variety of particular national reasons for exemptions, for example on 'cultural' grounds, where it is difficult, as with health regulations, to distinguish between protectionism and genuine non-economic motives.

The agreement provides explicitly for new general negotiations to be held within five years, and in some sectors these were to begin immediately. These were financial services and shipping, where there were serious disagreements at the end of the negotiations, and most offers were left provisional; basic telecommunications (telephone systems, etc.) where there was a basic division between those who had liberalised their national service and the rest; and labour movement: many developing countries see greater access here as the counterpart for opening their financial sectors.

The agreement on services lists the types of barrier which would be considered obstacles to access, and which a country must therefore specify in its offer on any service if it wishes to maintain them (Table 7.1). They are a mixture of restrictions analogous to NTBs on goods (quotas on suppliers or transactions), restrictions on labour, and restrictions on capital. There appear to be two possible problems: (i) mixing the various types of restriction may blur countries' perceptions of the economic costs and benefits of different types of restrictions; (ii) in a new area like services, there is a risk that listing the possible restrictions as clearly as this could provide the impulse and basis for detailed regulation, rather than for liberalisation of services (analogous to the spread of awareness of sophisticated anti-dumping methods, see Chapter 9). But securing agreement that these constitute barriers could reduce the type of disagreement found in early NTB analysis and negotiations.

Because of the importance of national regulation in services, the question of whether certain types of even non-discriminatory regulation constituted a barrier was part of the Uruguay Round negotiations. The US tried to include minimum common requirements in some services, notably in financial, in other words standards requiring in some cases better than national treatment (analogous to the requirements for intellectual property protection: see Chapter 8). The agreement to permit (almost) anything provided it is registered at this stage postponed the issue, but as such requirements spread in other parts of the trading system, they are likely also to appear in services. Enforcement has already gone partly in this direction: in countries which make offers the government will be responsible for ensuring that they are

Table 7.1 Specific Commitments on Services:
Market Access

1. With respect to market access through the modes of supply identified in Article I, each Member shall accord services and service suppliers of any other Member treatment no less favourable than provided for under the terms, limitations and conditions agreed and specified in its schedule.[1]

2. In sectors where market access commitments are undertaken, the measures which a Member shall not maintain or adopt either on the basis of a regional subdivision or on the basis of its entire territory, unless otherwise specified in its schedule, are defined as:

(a) limitations on the number of service suppliers whether in the form of numerical quotas, monopolies, exclusive service suppliers or the requirements of an economic needs test;

(b) limitations on the total value of service transactions or assets in the form of numerical quotas or the requirement of an economic needs test;

(d) limitations on the total number of service operations or on the total quantity of service output expressed in terms of designated numerical units in the form of quotas or the requirement of an economic needs test;[2]

(e) measures which restrict or require specific types of legal entity or joint venture through which a service supplier may supply a service; and

(f) limitations on the participation of foreign capital in terms of maximum percentage limit on foreign shareholding or the total value of individual or aggregate foreign investment.

Source: GATT 1994, *Final Act*

Notes:

1. If a Member undertakes a market access commitment in relation to the supply of service through the mode of supply referred to in paragraph 2 (a) of Article I and if the cross-border movement of capital is an essential part of the service itself, that Member is thereby committed to allow such movement of capital. If a Member undertakes a market access commitment in relation to the supply of a service through the mode of supply referred to in paragraph 2(c) of Article I, it is thereby committed to allow related transfers of capital into its territory.

2. Sub-paragraph 2(c) does not cover measures of a Member which limit inputs for the supply of services.

75

implemented, even if, as in many professions and some services, there are systems for regulations to be administered by a non-governmental body.

Characteristics of developing countries' offers

The usual problems of different degrees of disaggregation or coverage, found also in measuring non-tariff barriers to goods, apply. In the case of services, the fact that any number and any type of restriction is acceptable if listed also means that simply counting sectors may mean counting restrictions. There is also the possibility of general ('horizontal') restrictions covering all sectors, and the existence of the MFN exemption lists, some of which are themselves classified by sector. GATT (data from Secretariat) has disaggregated the commitments by detailed sub-sector and by type of commitment (Table 7.2; Appendix Tables A2 and A3 give additional data). The average share of the total possible commitments for developing countries was 15%, with Asia highest at 26% and Africa lowest at 10%.

Table 7.2 Commitments on market access for service activities (number of bound service activities and percentages)

Country Group	Number of Commitments	Share of maximum possible
By major country group:		
Developed economies	2470	61.4
Developing economies	1806	14.6
Transition economies	306	47.5
By region:		
North America	193	59.9
Latin America	738	15.3
Western Europe	2002	59.2
Central Europe	351	43.6
Africa	396	9.8
Middle East	106	16.5
Asia	796	26.0

Source: GATT Secretariat

Measured at a more aggregate level, in order to avoid some of the disaggregation problems, using only the 11 major sectors, the pattern seems to hold (Table 7.3). The African countries normally offered fewer than half the sectors (South Africa is exceptional, at 7), with some at only one (and the majority have still not submitted offers). The Latin American and more advanced Asian countries made offers in more than half the sectors, and even India and Pakistan offered 5, more than some African countries. Bangladesh and Sri Lanka were exceptionally low with only one sector. Brazil, which with India was the main opponent at the outset to including services in the Round, made offers in 7.

Table 7.3: Services: countries' offers of access, by section (regions and selected countries)

	Business	Commun	Constr.	Distrib	Educat	Environ	Finance	Health	Tour	Recr	Trans	Number of sectors	Length in pages	Without MFN exemptions
Industrial Countries														
Canada	X	X	X	X		X	X				X	7	84	
EC	X	X	X	X	X	X	X	X	X	X	X	11	95	
Japan	X	X	X	X	X	X	X	X	X	X	X	11	78	X
US	X	X	X	X	X	X	X	X	X	X	X	11	76	
S Africa	X	X	X	X			X		X		X	7		
Developing, Africa														
Ghana			X		X				X			3		X
Kenya	X	X					X		X		X	5		X
Mauritius		X							X			2	8	X
Nigeria		X					X		X		X	4	7	X
Zimbabwe		X					X		X			3	6	X
Latin America														
Costa Rica	X				X			X	X			4		
Jamaica	X				X		X	X	X	X	X	7	12	
Argentina	X	X	X	X			X		X		X	6	23	X
Brazil	X	X	X	X			X		X		X	7	24	
Chile	X	X					X		X		X	5	36	
Colombia	X	X	X	X			X		X			6	42	
Venezuela	X	X	X				X		X		X	6	22	
Mexico	X	X	X	X	X		X	X	X		X	9	57	

Asia

Table 7.3 continued.

	C1	C2	C3	C4	C5	C6	C7	C8	C9	C10	C11			
Pakistan	X		X			X		X	X			5	16	
Bangladesh									X			1	1	X
Indonesia	X	X					X	X	X	X	X	6	40	
India	X	X	X				X	X	X			5		
Korea	X	X	X	X	X	X			X		X	8	61	
Malaysia	X	X				X	X		X		X	6	50	
Thailand	X	X	X			X	X	X	X	X	X	7	52	
Sri Lanka									X			1	7	X
Philippines	X	X				X	X		X		X	5	37	
China	X	X	X			X	X		X		X	5	36	
Hong Kong	X	X	X	X		X	X	X	X	X	X	8	36	
Total	43	30	22	11	6	23	33	14	55	14	27			

Sectors

	C1	C2	C3	C4	C5	C6	C7	C8	C9	C10	C11
Africa	9	8	5	2	1	0	8	1	15	1	7
Asia	17	11	10	2	1	2	9	6	18	4	9
Latin America	17	11	9	7	4	0	16	7	22	9	11

Source: GATT 1994, Service Offers

There is a clear ranking in the MFN exemptions lists: many of the African countries, and Bangladesh and Sri Lanka among the Asian, submitted no exemptions. Those submitted by the Latin American countries were generally limited to regional or other group commitments, especially in transport. Almost all the major Asian countries, middle- and low-income, including Pakistan, Indonesia, the Philippines, India, Korea, and Hong Kong required reciprocity in financial, and often in other, services. China (which submitted an offer in spite of not yet being a member) demanded it in legal services. Some also had regional or other arrangements (e.g. acceptance of the UNCTAD liner code) in shipping. Because it will not be possible to declare exemptions without justification and agreement from the WTO at the time of the initial offer, the less developed countries which do not have lists now will find it more difficult to introduce discrimination later. The Latin American emphasis on regional groups is not surprising as these are much more common among those countries than in the other areas, and specifying them in detail in the offer means that they will not need to be examined under the new supervisory provisions for regional groups.

Almost all the developing countries have made offers in **tourism** (and this is frequently the single offer for those making only one). Most of the Latin American and Asian countries have also included **business services** (which includes professional services, and also computer services). Most of the Latin American countries have made offers in **financial services,** but both the Asian and the African countries are more closed. Among the Asian countries the more advanced have made offers, as has China. It is the East Asian countries which the US pressed most strongly during the Round. **Communications** is the only other area to have attracted a substantial number of offers, along with **construction** for the Asian countries. In **distribution,** as in financial services (the other service supplied most directly to the user), the Latin American countries have been, by a large margin, the most open. **Transport** is a sensitive area, because of the labour advantages of the developing countries and its important role in ensuring that traded goods can reach markets without uncompetitive costs or delays. (This was reflected in the MFN exemptions as well.) The offers that are made are, therefore, limited and hedged with restrictions. The **health** offers are frequently limited by requirements of national qualifications, while even the small number of **education** offers that have been made have (as in the EU offer) frequent nationality obligations. The least common, **environmental,** basically means local services, and without labour movement it is difficult to see how most countries could trade in it, except perhaps in border areas.

As suggested above, the **African** offers are, fairly consistently, limited, even in countries which have been opening their trade in goods. In many cases, including Zimbabwe, Ghana and Mauritius, African countries further reduce their offers at both general and sectoral level by restrictions on investment and migration. In the remaining countries, labour, but not capital, is restricted. In almost all cases, the offers favour managerial and expert labour, not unskilled. For Zimbabwe basic telecommunications are excluded, but the financial sector is substantially opened. Ghana's specific offers are restrictive. Kenya's general section also excludes labour, but its sectoral offers are more open. Mauritius' offer on communications is strong, but, perhaps surprisingly for a small country normally judged to be relatively open (and one which hoped to become a regional centre for trading and financial services), its only other offer is in tourism, and this is subject to more restrictions on investment and migration than that of many other countries. Nigeria is perhaps an exception to the general restrictiveness of African offers, although it has included only four sectors. It has general restrictions only on migration. It excludes the basic telecommunications services, but its financial and tourism offers are relatively strong, with its transport offer mainly limited by UNCTAD-type restrictions to protect the share of Nigerian shipping.

This closer examination of individual countries thus confirms the impression from the aggregate data that the African offers do not offer much access for other countries, perhaps particularly not for regional trade as many of the sectoral openings are on relatively advanced services (advanced telecommunications or financial) or in tourism where most specialist suppliers are either from industrial countries or from Asia. But for the sectors in which they do make offers, the detail is much less than in the offers of the industrial countries or of the Latin American and more advanced Asian countries, presumably reflecting less advanced domestic regulatory regimes.[27] This, like their limited use of MFN exemptions, could provide the clearest evidence on the results of introducing international rules and liberalisation of services at an early stage of development.

As in Africa, in **Latin America** there seems little relationship between the countries generally considered open and the extent of the services offers. Argentina and Venezuela, unusually among the major countries, do not restrict investment, although they have general restrictions on labour, apart from managerial. Argentina's six sectoral offers are in the usual sectors (but exclude transport), and are subject to detailed restrictions. Brazil has general regulation on investment, the form of 'commercial presence', as well as on labour. Chile gives detailed requirements on the criteria for investment to establish 'commercial presence', which include not only the financial requirements common in many countries, but its contribution to development, efficiency, and a long list of other national interests. Labour is restricted to managerial. It offers relatively few sectors compared with other Latin American countries, and these offers are substantially qualified. Mexico retains (as it did under NAFTA) some restrictions on foreign investment by sector and the usual restrictions on labour, but it offers all sectors except the two least traded, environmental and recreation. Although it only offers four sectors, Costa Rica includes two of the least often opened, health and education, probably reflecting its programme of trying to become a major provider of both to foreign users. In its general restrictions, it includes only labour, but the sectoral offers do not bind it from imposing restrictions on commercial presence. Its offers on education and health include restrictions on nationality. Jamaica has only minor restrictions on capital, in addition to those on labour, but its sectoral offers frequently demand joint ventures. Colombia's foreign investment restrictions are relatively limited, and it has made offers in a range of sectors.

Subject to various restrictions (but not prohibitions) on the role of foreign capital, the Latin American countries offer opportunities to other developing countries as well as to the industrial. Their own service sectors may benefit from access to the Colombian market in sectors like distribution, tourism and transport, and perhaps also in finance, although this last may be more important for industrial country suppliers. The very detailed regulation, however, suggests that in many cases the offers are merely setting out the present position, and therefore any 'opening' effect will come only from making the conditions more transparent.

---

27. As a rough measure, the African offers are typically under 10 pages, the Latin American 20-40, the Asian up to 50 or 60, and the US, EU, and Japan 75-100. The exceptions include Mexico, which is substantially longer, probably reflecting its greater experience in negotiating on services in preparation for NAFTA, as well as its relative development, and in Asia Bangladesh (1) and Sri Lanka (7).

This could, however, be an important impulse to Latin American integration in the 1990s, given the long history of relatively little regional trade and contact, and the new interest in regional blocs.

Among the south **Asian** countries, Bangladesh and Sri Lanka made offers only in tourism. For Bangladesh, this is limited to five-star hotels. This access is not new. In spite of the limited scope of its sectoral offer, Sri Lanka specifies general (tight) restrictions on foreign investment and labour in its offer. It is unlikely that its offer gives new opportunities. Pakistan also records restrictions on the share of foreign investment and controls on labour, except managerial; and these are the principal controls in its sectoral offers. Although India includes only general restrictions on labour, almost all its sectoral offers are declared to be unbound; like Pakistan, however, it offers more sectors (five) than most of the African countries (although few by Latin American or more advanced Asian standards). This could reflect greater experience, and confidence, in domestic regulatory regimes, although the detail of restrictions is still substantially less than among the Latin Americans or other Asians.

The Philippine and Chinese offers are also at an intermediate level, with general restrictions on foreign ownership as well as labour. The Philippine restrictions tend to give a large role for discretionary government approval of establishment, while the Chinese, at general and sectoral level, are among the most detailed. Indonesia restricts capital and labour at the national level, and also offers only a limited number of sectors. The sectoral regulation includes a significant number of quota-type limits on numbers of companies which can be established.

Among the more advanced countries, Malaysia and Thailand have detailed and restrictive regulation at the general level of foreign capital and labour. Although Malaysia has made offers in only a limited number of the most commonly offered areas (plus health), these are mainly long lists of highly specific regulations, suggesting that even these are not openings, but records of present restrictions.

Hong Kong and Korea have made offers in the largest number of sectors among Asian countries. Hong Kong has no general restrictions, but its sectoral offers normally imply restrictions on labour, except managerial; in other aspects, they tend to be open. This probably does not, however, reflect any major changes. Korea has general restrictions on investment, and the usual special treatment for managers. These are supplemented by exceptionally detailed regulation at the sectoral level.

Market opening in the industrial countries

Measured by number of commitments, the **EU** and US both include about 60% of the classifications (Table 7.2). The EU has made MFN exemptions for a variety of regional or bilateral arrangements, for example those of Denmark with the other Nordic countries. It has some regional transport arrangements and a range of 'cultural' ones, on the basis of nationality or language. There are also some restrictions on some professions in some countries. It also lists some reciprocal agreements in finance and transport. Some restrictions (including those based on language, for example by Portugal) imply special entry privileges for a few developing countries, but most are with other European countries.

Japan has no MFN exemptions.

The **United States** has one of the longest lists of MFN restrictions, with many to be applied on an unspecified, and thus discretionary, basis (or according to US legislation, with the relevant provisions not registered). These are in a wide range of sectors, and include provisions on labour movement, on ownership of land, and some which vary by state. Some in transport and finance are reciprocal, and specify some of the agreements on which they are based.

The **US** has detailed regulations in its 'horizontal' conditions for types of specialist or professional staff which are permitted to enter, and declares a wide range of subsidies to individual services unbound. The provisions both here and on many of the sectoral offers again include a number of requirements imposed by individual states. On communications, distribution, and education its offers are relatively free of restrictions on access (except on 'natural persons'), although many have limitations on national treatment, with differences in fees, etc., for non-US suppliers. Financial services are limited, and made explicitly subject to the renegotiation. The regulation in many cases is on a state basis. Health services are restricted in some cases. Travel has some restrictions on commercial operations by official offices, which might increase the costs of developing countries officially promoting themselves.

The **EU's** general restrictions apply to public sector operations, some types of investment, and labour entry. In specialised and professional services there are a wide range of restrictions, and although there are fewer on some of the less advanced services, the general restrictions on movement of labour would protect these from full-scale competition. As in the US, in these and other services there are also a range of country restrictions. Communications, construction and particularly distribution all have restrictions in some countries, largely because of public sector intervention, but the requirements also include nationality. For distribution, there are also frequently quotas on numbers of establishments. Education has nationality conditions in many countries. Like the US, the financial services section is made subject to the renegotiation, and there are frequent national conditions. Health and tourism services are subject effectively to quotas on establishments and some nationality conditions. Transport is frequently restricted.

Japan's horizontal conditions are entirely on the entry of labour. Combined with requirements of commercial presence for many of the principal business services, including law and accountancy, this effectively controls some sectors completely. The communications offer is very specific, and limited. Construction is more open, but of course subject to the limitations on labour. Distribution services are subject to an exceptionally long list of exceptions. Financial services are subject both to the renegotiation and a general exemption for 'prudential reasons'. Again, commercial presence is frequently required. Health, tourism and recreation are generally subject mainly to the general restraints on labour. International transport is restricted. It has reduced restrictions on investments and some types of insurance, and on legal services (Japan, 1994).

Results

The principal measurable effect is on the information now available to all countries about the opportunities and restrictions in their potential trading partners. This does not extend to sectors in which an offer has not been made, and this is a significant weakness in international regulation of services relative to goods (Sauvé, 1994). The actual gains in access are impossible to measure in the absence of similar data for 1986, before the Round.

Developing countries with low labour costs should be expected to increase their exports if a labour-intensive sector like services is liberalised. This will certainly be true of services where access under one of the first two modes of supply is sufficient: cross-border or consumption in the supplying country. The most advanced developing countries have been increasing their investment in service industries in industrial countries, but, except to facilitate the marketing of their own services, they seem likely to have little systematic advantage in these. It is a natural progression for growing companies, and will be assisted by any general liberalisation, but offers no particular prospect of significant increases in market share. They would have an advantage if the 'movement of natural persons', i.e. migration,were liberalised, but this is not found in the offers, including their own. They are probably at a disadvantage to the extent that it is less likely that they will supply the professional and managerial labour which is normally granted at least limited access, and their own salary structures suggest that they have a much smaller cost advantage in this. As in goods, the restrictions tend to be higher on the low-cost and intermediate labour which they export than on the more sophisticated (the equivalent of high-technology goods) characteristic of the industrial countries.[28] Migration is, however, one of the points on the programme for immediate discussion. (This consistent discrimination between types of labour is another point where an analysis which could consider the distribution of effects within countries would be desirable.) The most frequently included areas, tourism, business services, and finance, probably favour developed countries, although in some business services developing countries have been able to build up exportable services, e.g. in publishing and data processing.

The need to specify now all MFN exemptions and all limitations on the services which are scheduled, without the possibility of adding to them as they become more experienced in using, providing and trading services, has, not surprisingly, made the least developed countries very cautious in offering individual sectors, although many have effectively given up the possibility of making MFN exemptions. The lack of differential treatment for developing countries may have hindered the process of maximising the level of offers. Although it might have been possible to make detailed, but unbound, registration of current regulation (as India has done), this option seems to have been little used. Although developing countries can create an effect equivalent to protection from imports (where reciprocity has not been specified) through not making offers and using the offers of those which have made them on an MFN basis, there is no provision for an equivalent of preferences. Industrial countries could have created this, through appropriate scheduling of MFN exemptions, but with minor

---

28. It is tempting to suggest, by analogy with national anti-discrimination legislation, that developing countries could argue that the discriminatory provisions on types of labour were an implicit violation of MFN treatment because they are inherently more likely to suffer from them, but their own adoption of similar rules would seriously weaken their position.

exceptions they have not done so.

Services are, on the basis of unreliable data, perhaps 15% of the exports of developing countries. Their share in world trade in services, in contrast to their performance in manufactures, appears to have been falling, although, at 18%, it is still similar to its share in total world trade (UNCTAD,1994 *Supplement*). A 10% rise from the opening of markets could raise their exports by 1.5%, large relative to some of the other effects summarised in Chapter 6. In terms of sectors, the Asian countries' services exports are largest in some of the most controlled services, like transport and finance, where some opening, and therefore some new prospects, can be found. The typical Latin American services (notably tourism) face fewer controls, but this was already true. Africa has much lower values of all services; again travel is important. Given the type of services in which they trade, the Asian countries will probably benefit most. The African countries have least to gain, in the short run. Services are most important, in aggregate, for some of the smallest countries (Table 7.4), but in many cases it is tourism, where gains are unlikely to be great, which is the principal service.

Table 7.4: Share of commercial services in total foreign-exchange earnings (merchandise plus commercial services) of selected developing economies, 1992

Above 80%	Antigua and Barbuda, Lesotho
60.1 – 80%	Barbados, Maldives, Dominican Republic. Egypt, Cyprus, Santa Lucia, Gambia
40.1 – 60%	Mozambique, Jamaica, Belize, Kuwait, Benin, Kenya, Paraguay, Dominica, Haiti
20 – 40%	Malta, St. Vincent and the Grenadines, Philippines, Turkey, Senegal, El Salvador, Togo, Mauritius, Israel, Costa Rica, Guatemala, Morocco, Madagascar, Tanzania, Uruguay, Sierra Leone, Tunisia, Swaziland, Rwanda, Mexico, Thailand, Singapore, Sri Lanka

Note: Countries within each range are listed in descending order of the share of commercial services. "Commercial services" refer only to cross-border service transactions recorded in the balance-of-payments by the country in question; not covered are service transactions by non-national service providers located in the domestic market.

Source: GATT, 1994 *Access*.

As has happened with negotiations on goods in the half century since the founding of GATT, it is likely that services negotiations will become more standardised with greater experience and information. The emphasis on regulating the supplier rather than the service has led GATT to argue that the services agreement is basically about investment. In practice, this has become true, but it is not clear that it needs to be so. Little progress has been made on liberalising movement in labour, but this was because of countries' unwillingness rather than because of lack of scope in the form of the agreement. But there are some clear common elements in the patterns of restrictions, apparent even in the cursory summaries here, and they are not restricted to those on labour. It is a mistake to assume that there is no possibility of negotiating about services rather than suppliers. There are significant numbers of countries with, for example, quota-type restrictions on numbers of providers and additional nationality restrictions reinforcing residence or local qualification restrictions. It might be possible in future negotiations (and perhaps through a re-arrangement of the offers) to make these common types of control more explicit and consider some across all services, as tariffs or non-tariff barriers are negotiated in goods. It may make a more useful start than the present distinction among the forms of provision, which in practice tends to become detail on investment and labour. The inclusion of labour movement as one of the four areas for immediate further negotiations is a step in this direction. Such an approach may be particularly useful for those developing countries which do not yet have detailed national regulations to adapt to international regulation.

8. Trade related provisions of the settlement

Government procurement

The agreement on opening government purchases which was reached following the Tokyo Round was a 'plurilateral agreement', in other words GATT members could choose whether to join it. A revised agreement was negotiated during (technically not as a part of) the Uruguay Round, and this will come into effect in 1996 and have the same status in the WTO. The new agreement includes extension to some services, including construction;[29] to other levels of government, at the equivalent of states or counties and some large cities (previously only national governments were covered); and to five public utilities: water, ports, airports, electricity, and urban transport. GATT estimated that this could extend its coverage by a factor of 10, but this is very uncertain because, as in the services agreement, countries have the option of deciding to which levels of government and which utilities they will apply these extensions.

There will be little direct effect on developing countries because only Israel and Korea have signed the agreement.[30] In principle there could be some diversion in countries which have followed the practice of permitting some foreign bidding, but with a price advantage for national bidders; by receiving national treatment, other members of the agreement will be placed at an advantage relative to non-members. The new agreement, however, is also intended to encourage more developing countries to join, apparently principally by providing assistance in analysing the benefits to a particular country of joining.

Trade-related intellectual property (TRIPs)

Copyright, patent, and other forms of protecting 'intellectual property' have not been treated in the past as trade (or even trade-related) issues. They have had their own international negotiations, notably through the World Intellectual Property Organisation, or been subject to bilateral agreements. The first international trade agreement to include them was NAFTA. They were brought into the Uruguay Round initially because exports from some South-East Asian countries of counterfeit goods, ranging from software to designer clothing, were seen as a growing problem, while pharmaceutical companies, especially in the US, had long seen local production of their products, without payment of licence fees and justified as national health policies, as a serious cost to their potential trade. If these could be treated as trade issues, this opened up the possibility of using trade sanctions, whether bilateral or multilateral through GATT, if domestic enforcement mechanisms within the offending countries do not meet the agreed standards or are ineffectual.

The agreement thus had to go beyond the traditional concept of national treatment: equality with local producers, to setting minimum acceptable standards for protection, and thus necessarily its effects would go well beyond those goods and services actually traded. In

---

29. The services agreement itself is part of the WTO, and therefore applies to all member companies, but any offers under, for example, construction there would not apply to public procurement for countries not also joining the additional agreement.

30. The developed members are the EU, Austria, Finland, Sweden, Norway, Switzerland, Japan, the US and Canada.

addition to the basic argument, that authors, inventors, etc., should receive payment, the argument was used that foreign investors would not transfer technology to countries which did not offer it protection. This would become increasingly important as countries move up to more high-technology exports. It is not clear why this should be seen as giving an economic need for international agreement when it is the country's own access to technology that would be damaged. But the basic reason for including TRIPs was not trade or development, but to ensure a 'just return' to technical innovation. Like the concept of helping countries 'damaged' by reforms, it introduces a new criterion to trade negotiations, although not to international negotiations. The IFC has found evidence that some industries claim to be influenced; others do not, and it is more important for transferring research departments than investment for production. Gould and Gruben (1994) have found that in open (but not necessarily in closed) economies there is a correlation between growth and protection of intellectual property because of an enhanced premium on rapid innovation and rapid access to the most modern technology. If, however, a country suffers loss through not offering protection, the remedy of altering its own legislation is available to it, regardless of what other countries may do; it could be argued that any one country would gain more advantage if other countries do not offer the same benefit. Some of the South-East Asian countries which were particularly targeted by the US in the negotiations were among the major recipients of foreign investment at the same time.

It could be that the growing importance of high-technology, innovative industries in investment in developing countries had made the issue a more general problem, but this change was most characteristic of Japanese investment and in sectors like electronics. In contrast the pressure to include the issue came from the US, and from the pharmaceuticals producers and the more traditional computer producers, suggesting that it was the result of traditional protectionism by (comparatively) old industries.

The agreement requires countries to accept the substance of existing international conventions on copyright (the Berne convention) and on patents (the Paris Convention). It thus opens the range of GATT/WTO dispute settlement and enforcement mechanisms including trade-offs with other trade issues to those with any complaints under these, apparently including violations which began before the UR settlement, provided these are still in dispute, i.e. up to 100 years of existing disputes, since the signing of the Berne Convention in 1886). In principle, there should be no conflict between its provisions and those of the existing conventions: the WTO agreement is declared to prevail in any conflicts of competence. It adds to the existing Conventions by clarifying that computer programs and some data bases are covered by patent provisions, and by increasing the range of types of protection, for example on films and unauthorised (and uncompensated) recording, and by specifying the minimum periods of protection. In accordance with the original justification for including the issue as trade-related, it requires minimum standards for trademark protection, including specification of origin. On patents, it allows countries to exclude certain types of process for reasons of national policy, but specifically includes among products to be patentable the controversial one of plant varieties (with the option of protecting by patents, by the method given by the existing international agreement, the UPOV, International Union for the Protection of New Varieties of Plants, or by any equivalent method).[31] Integrated circuits and industrial designs are to be protected (although for only 10 years; patents get 20).

What is most surprising about this agreement is that, in spite of its marginal relationship to the traditional concerns of GATT and to the negotiating interests of most of the participants in the Uruguay Round, its scope and strength go well beyond those in other sectors. It even specifies minimum legal and administrative procedure requirements to be used for enforcement. Special treatment for developing countries is much more limited than in the goods and services agreements: while industrial countries must conform within a year, middle-income developing countries (and the former centrally planned countries) have 5 years and the least developed 11 years (this last can be extended by the Council which is to supervise the agreement if a country makes a 'duly motivated' request). In some cases where there is no current legislation, the middle-income countries have 10 years, but pharmaceutical and some chemical products can start to apply for patents immediately, receiving the protection as soon as the adjustment period is completed. There are increased obligations to license the use of technology.

For developing countries which are still net importers of technology, the traditional choice was, as it was for their industrial country predecessors, between buying technology (and offering appropriate protection) and minimising costs by finding alternative means of access to it. These included foreign investment (from those investors not deterred by lack of protection), hiring external advisers, or direct copying, or stealing.

The extra costs the agreement imposes are of two types. The costs of being forced to pay for technology would be expected to fall principally on the low- to middle-income countries. The higher-income countries are approaching the point at which they have their own technology to export and protect. It was these, led by Brazil and India, which most strongly opposed inclusion of this issue in the Round. Seven years later, Brazil may now be moving up out of this group, with its own computer industry. Many other countries have signed even stricter bilateral agreements on intellectual property with the US under threat of unilateral trade action, while others have altered their national laws. Mexico, with the prospect of NAFTA restrictions as well as the GATT agreement, passed its own legislation protecting patents in 1991.

In these circumstances, it is difficult to know how many countries can be said to be directly affected by this type of cost. The effect could even be positive if multilateral agreement protects them from more onerous bilateral treaties. (The agreement did not , however, have the effect of reducing pressure for bilateral agreements immediately: the US was still demanding a bilateral treaty from Argentina in May 1994.) Some countries, however, are likely to be affected on patents, including those in South Asia (which have not in general signed such agreements; India has not signed even the Paris Convention) and perhaps other

---

31. It does not, contrary to allegations by some pressure groups, forbid farmers to replant seeds from their own crops, and since it does not act retrospectively, it does not raise the costs of existing plants. GATT, at least (Sutherland, *Times* 1994), accepts that local sales are also impossible to police. The costs of purchases of new varieties could be increased, as suppliers of seeds would be required to pay their developers, and there is the risk that existing varieties, whether because they became less popular or because they were less profitable, could become more difficult to acquire.

88

Latin American. Countries with major pharmaceutical production by unlicensed local producers, such as India and Argentina, are examples. On the other hand if, as suggested above, protecting technology is more of an advantage in open than closed economies, the move in this direction by many middle-income countries could help to explain their reduced resistance to the TRIPs agreement. It is noteworthy, however, that it is principally external observers who have seen and warned about the costs of paying for technology at an early stage of development. Most of the governments signing the agreement did not oppose it.

The other costs, of introducing the required legal and administrative mechanisms, will be highest for the least developed countries. The agreement suggests official technical assistance and private investment would be appropriate, but offers no source of finance for providing or encouraging these.

The effects on the nature of the international system may be broader. Like the framework for financial services, the agreement adds to the concept of 'national treatment': 'that treatment which many nations consider satisfactory'. But it also sets a precedent for twisting the concept of 'trade-related' to cover subjects where some countries feel that others' enforcement mechanisms are inadequate and that trade instruments could be an effective substitute. This opens the way for a variety of new international issues to come under the WTO, rather than under other international regulatory bodies (existing or new). It is not clear whether even the new structure of the WTO is capable of such unlimited extension.

Trade-related investment measures (TRIMs)

TRIMs faded into the background during the Round, leaving four anodyne pages in the Final Act. This was partly because some of the issues related to investment were incorporated into other parts of the agreement, including services and TRIPs, but changes in attitudes and in the flows of investment probably also contributed. More industrial countries were receiving investment, and some had always regulated it (the exceptions incorporated into the EU services offer to meet French demands are powerful examples) and others felt a growing need to regulate (pressure from the US on sensitive purchases; intervention by the UK on foreign banks). In contrast, more developing countries were liberalising their own provisions, as part of their trade liberalisation or because of growing confidence in their ability to exploit the advantages of foreign investment without suffering from its potential power (notably in South-East Asia, but also in Latin America). As in TRIPs, a growing network of bilateral and regional agreements was also leading to at least partial opening (for example, Mexico in NAFTA). The OAU concluded (OAU, 1994) that the new obligations might not be contrary to present trends in national legislation.

The principal targets of those who wanted to include TRIMs in the Uruguay Round were regulations on use of local inputs and on exports.

The TRIMs section deals only with investment related to traded goods (services investments are covered in the services section, and thus subject to national offers). Its principal requirements are national treatment and prohibition of export or import restrictions, but these are specified as compliance with the existing Articles III and XI. Effectively, therefore, it is merely confirming and perhaps clarifying existing obligations: it adds an 'llustrative list' of measures that would be inconsistent with these articles. Developing countries can have temporary exemptions under the usual balance-of-payments protection conditions. There are further exceptions for not only existing arrangements with companies but arrangements with companies that might compete with those which already have arrangements. Countries are required to notify GATT of those measures which they are using, and to remove them: within 2 years for industrial countries, 5 for middle income and 7 for the least developed. The list of measures inconsistent with Articles III and XI includes requirements to use local inputs or to limit the use of imports or specifying export requirements.

These requirements were well known to be contrary to GATT before the Uruguay Round. Countries whose investors faced them chose not to take them to dispute settlement, presumably because maintaining the investments and good relations with the erring government was more important than avoiding the restriction. It is not clear that repeating that they are illegal, and indeed *de facto* legitimising them during the set adjustment periods, will make investing companies or their governments more interested in making formal complaints. The agreement does not mention restrictions of foreign ownership of certain sectors or of land, the kind seen most often as problems in bilateral disputes, and observed in the qualifications in the services offers. Thus, the agreement did not formally represent any extension of GATT into control of investment (in contrast to the services agreement or the regulatory extension embodied in the TRIPs agreement). There are, however, provisions for further negotiations to open within five years.

Preshipment inspection (PSI)

In the last 10 years many developing countries have brought in international agents to check the price and/or quality of their imports before they are shipped from the exporting country. This was intended to supplement normal customs procedures (in at least one case, Indonesia, it entirely replaced the customs service) and reduce the risks of exporters not meeting normal quality standards or over-pricing; developing countries were assumed to be vulnerable as inexperienced buyers. This was not an imaginary problem: over-pricing to the OPEC countries in the late 1970s had been large and conspicuous enough to find its way into the specification of trade models, as well as into the consciousness of importers. It was also a deterrent to the use of over- (or under-) pricing to transfer funds to low-tax countries, profits beyond the reach of a possibly unstable country, and payments to possibly corrupt customs services. Exporters, particularly inexperienced ones, objected to it, ostensibly on the grounds of delay and cost.

The Uruguay Round agreement starts, in the preamble to this agreement, from the assumption that only developing countries use it. This is unusual, if not unique, and it is not obvious why it is even relevant. Like the agreement on TRIMs, it is phrased as clarifying existing GATT obligations, not instituting new ones. It does not forbid PSI but it requires non-discriminatory and transparent implementation, and commercial confidentiality. In terms of more explicit regulations, it sets out that exporters should not be required to supply extra information and sets a time limit for the inspection. The principal new requirement seems to be the limits on which prices can be used for comparison of export prices: not prices for products for other markets or from other countries or home prices in the importing country, and not the costs of production, for example. A separate dispute settlement mechanism is provided, but the normal GATT mechanisms remain available.

This was another issue which was much more controversial at the beginning of the Round than at the end. Since then, it has become less controversial, partly because greater familiarity has reduced exporters' fears of unfamiliar procedures, and partly because standard procedures have already emerged.

This Agreement is explicitly targeted at the developing countries and therefore intended to restrict them. Presumably an industrial country would be subject to the same rules, but this is not mentioned. In other Decisions and Agreements of the Round the least developed countries are considered a separate group, not a sub-category of 'developing countries', so the Agreement presumably does not apply to them, but again this is not stated. The list of excluded comparative prices is sufficient to eliminate all possible comparisons for a one-off major purchase of equipment, while more standard goods do not usually need or get PSI. (There are typically minimum values above which inspection is required.) As with the TRIMs provisions, it is not clear that a company with long-term relations with an importer would want to take a dispute to settlement, and the normal remedy would be not to accept another order.

9. The new regulatory framework

Trade Policy Reviews

Since 1986, new sources of information about trade and trade policy have transformed countries' awareness of trade policy, and the possibilities of a systematic approach to trade regulation. From its foundation, GATT had necessarily had full records of all the tariffs 'bound' by its member countries, and formal derogations like the MFA. Starting at the end of the 1970s it and UNCTAD started to collect data on non-tariff barriers (hitherto records had only been kept irregularly, even within national governments, and comparative data only by unofficial sources). There was also a series on developments in trade, available but not formally published, and some information about trade in the IMF's *Annual Report on Exchange Restrictions*. From the mid-1980s, first UNCTAD, then GATT began to use this information in some publications, although still without regular published series. The decision to include services in the Uruguay Round made the lack of any regular official information on services an obvious gap, previously filled by balance-of-payments data from the IMF, limited national information, and conflicting data from private sources. The negotiations in the services group revealed much about how these markets actually operated, and which countries had active interests in which services, and GATT began to publish data in its annual review of trade, while countries improved their own efforts to compile such data.

At what was intended to be the mid-term review of the negotiations of the Uruguay Round, in 1988, a system of GATT reports on countries' trade policy regimes was approved and immediately introduced. At first these were described as purely fact-finding exercises, which would not criticise policies or make formal findings that any were contrary to GATT rules. Preparing comprehensive descriptions of countries' trade regimes and presenting them for discussion to the country's government and to the GATT Council, and then publishing them could not avoid giving to trading partners and others information which could be the basis for criticisms, implicitly backed by the authority of GATT.

Under the programme, each country is reviewed (large countries at two-year intervals, middle and smaller countries at four and six years). The first reviews accorded with the neutral model. But by the time second reviews were reached, the procedure had acquired respectability, and the GATT teams could not simply repeat the information in the first. The result was an increasingly critical and judgmental approach. As this was applied first to the EU and the US (the first countries to come up for second reviews), it became acceptable before any developing country could be faced with it. It has become increasingly important and has been extended from comments on protective measures to discussion of trade policies and their effects on growth. It is noteworthy that the officials responsible for the reports at the time they were initiated argued strongly that they had to remain at least formally purely descriptive, however they might be used; now the view is that such a limitation would be impractical.

The coverage of the reports will also be extended. Services, intellectual property and the other new areas in the WTO will become parts of the report. As with the initial reports on trade in goods, the first task for these will be compiling the necessary information. They have been, and are expected to remain, based entirely on official information and contacts, reflecting GATT's government and country approach to trade.

One recent change to the system could weaken the role of developing countries, and implicitly contribute to GATT and the developing countries seeing the reports more as judgements on the countries reviewed. The obligation of the country being reviewed to produce its own report has been removed. This is presented as easing the burden, but the country reports have in some cases (cf. GATT, 1992 *Bangladesh*) been used to present complaints about other countries' obstacles to trade and justifications of their own policies. While this may not have been the purpose of the Reviews, it is a useful way of encouraging countries to participate in the system, and provides extra information for the users. As the developed countries are unlikely to give up their right of reply, this could produce a two-tier system, suggesting, however unintentionally, a discriminatory approach by the WTO, under which reports on developed countries were collaborative while those on developing countries were *de haut en bas*.

The recent, informal, GATT proposal of some unspecified type of co-operation with the IMF's country reports reinforces this impression. These IMF country reports have, *de facto*, long been different in their approaches to developed and developing countries, and they have evolved very differently from the GATT reports. They are explicitly intended to judge countries' compliance with IMF requirements; they are not subject to semi-public discussion; and they are not published. These differences and the nature of the reports reflect a basic difference between the organisations: the IMF has direct financial rewards and sanctions to offer; GATT (or the WTO) has only the authority given by its role as expert. All action must be taken on the initiative of a member and any sanctions must be taken or rewards paid for by members (or other institutions).

Dispute settlement

The major reform to dispute settlement under the Uruguay Round is that the findings by the panels which act as tribunals are now binding, unless they are challenged on a point of law. Previously, all stages depended on consensus, including, remarkably, the acceptance by the defending country of the ruling. Although there was minor strengthening at the time of the mid-term Review, this was more than offset during the Round by the growing number of members (led by the EU) which used the excuse of waiting for the outcome of the Round to postpone acceptance of rulings. (These delays were applied to disputes about existing obligations on questions which were not likely to be changed by the settlement.) There was also scope for procedural delays and objections at each stage of a dispute (the first disputes under the procedure adopted in 1989 were coming to the GATT Council in 1992–3). Countries (led by the US) also continued to make their own judgement that a trading partner had violated the rules, and take sanctions without bringing GATT into the dispute.

Under the old system, as it had evolved from the beginning of the GATT, countries which could not resolve a dispute bilaterally requested the GATT Council to appoint a panel of experts (normally from outside GATT) who then presented their decision to the Council, which could choose whether to adopt it. The remedies available were altering the policy or action about which the complaint had been made or compensating the complaining country, directly or through an alternative concession. In principle, as a last resort, the Council could recommend retaliation by the injured country, but this (the most common threat by countries acting outside the GATT) was only formally authorised once (Pescatore, 1993).

Under the new provisions, countries are still required to have formal bilateral consultations before requesting a dispute panel, but there are time limits laid down (30 days) for entering such consultations; the WTO must be informed from the beginning of the process. The negotiations have a time limit (60 days), after which the complaining country can refer the dispute to the WTO. The General Council of the WTO will continue to act as the Dispute Settlement Body (DSB), and to appoint panels and receive their reports. Under the old rules, the establishment of a panel had originally been discretionary, although the practice had become increasingly automatic. The 'Right to a Panel' is now prescribed, unless the Council votes against it, although it can be postponed once. Again there are time limits at all stages: 30 days to choose the panel, 20 days for the countries involved to approve it (in the absence of approval, the Director-General of WTO can appoint), and a maximum of six months to complete its report. The Report is then automatically adopted unless rejected by the DSB within 60 days, with the only limitation a possibility of appeal to a standing committee (again of outsiders) with a time limit of 60 days. Again, its report stands unless voted down by the Council.

If a complaint has been upheld, the offending country has only 20 days to agree on a remedy. In the absence of this, the complaining country can request permission for retaliation. In principle, the retaliation should be linked to the sector in which the dispute occurred. If this is not possible, it can be a different but related sector within the same Agreement (i.e. goods or services or TRIPs, etc.). If this is not possible, it can be in another Agreement.

All these reforms go to meet the problems of delays and the possibility of avoiding remedies which characterised the old system. More important, they remove (formally at least) the opportunity for a country to prevent a report from being adopted. It makes the approach to disputes more legalistic and less modelled on trade negotiations, with their emphasis on consensus and bargaining. It is now necessary for the WTO Council (and thus the countries not involved) to take action to reject a Panel report, not positive action to accept it.

There are declarations within the new procedure that there will be special treatment for developing countries, but in practice this is limited to reconfirming the possibility under the old rules of extending the period during which the Panel must report or providing faster remedies. Countries are expected to exercise 'due constraint' before they bring complaints against the least developed countries, but again without formal limitation of their rights. Until the late 1980s most disputes were between industrial countries, with some actions against developing countries. Developing countries have now started to use the procedure themselves, and the reduction of the need for positive approval of a panel's findings, and thus, perhaps, of the role of bargaining, could increase their confidence in using it against more powerful countries.

The effect of the reforms should not be exaggerated: even with all the loopholes available legally under the old system, countries still used unauthorised ones as well, notably unjustified postponing of implementation, bilateral action, and simply rejecting a finding. Enforcement continues to depend entirely on the complaining country's ability and willingness to take action itself. If it is not a major trading partner of its opponent, this may not be effective. There is no provision for action by other countries and GATT has no powers itself against a non-complying country. This will always limit the usefulness of the procedure for a small or low-income country acting against a larger one, and make such countries themselves more vulnerable to effective action if a developed country complains successfully about them. One possible answer to this problem if several countries had the same complaint, is for them to take joint action and secure permission to retaliate. There is now explicit provision for this.

The long-term effectiveness of the new procedures will depend crucially on whether they can build up users' confidence in the initial years, avoiding major delays or other procedural faults, and without large numbers of countries continuing to ignore the findings. Two potential problems are obvious. The new areas which have been brought into the WTO not only increase the scope of issues eligible for the procedure, but are particularly likely to generate disputes as countries learn how to interpret their new obligations and rights. The only mitigating factor suggested against this is that governments may choose not to bring cases unless they are certain of their position, because the early settlements in each subject will create a body of case law which will become the precedents for the future. The other problem is the backlog of disputes on issues that remain unresolved, some already subjected to the GATT procedure, but where findings were not implemented; others where the complainants may have deliberately chosen to wait to use the more effective WTO procedure. An obvious example between developing countries in Latin America and the EU is their complaint about the quota system for Latin American bananas. This system was instituted to protect the traditional suppliers in the ACP countries. Two panels have sat, ruling against the pre- and the post-1992 EU arrangements; their findings were rejected by the EU. Since then a GATT working group has challenged the whole Lomé arrangement for special treatment for selected developing countries (as discussed in Chapter 2). If the new disputes system is challenged in its early years by an exceptionally large number of serious disputes, including some where countries have already shown a willingness to defy rulings, it could lose its credibility very rapidly.

The new stronger system provoked opposition in the US and EU. The US added a procedure for decisions in which it is involved to be reviewed by US judges, with provision for them to report back to Congress, if they find three decisions within five years to be 'unjust'. In itself, this does not challenge GATT/WTO authority, provided that 'unjust' is interpreted as contrary to WTO procedures, not contrary to the evidence or to US economic interests. It would be a problem if it was used to justify taking unilateral measures or if, by making the option of withdrawing from the organisation seem a more immediate threat, it reduced the confidence advantages of defined rules and procedures (de Jonquières, 1994). It has been suggested that the EU should remove GATT/WTO rules from being directly applicable in the European Court of Justice. They were removed from national courts (in 1972) on the grounds that GATT regulations were more like negotiations than legal requirements, given the possibilities of derogations and need for consensus on any enforcement arising out of disputes, rather than automatic implementation (van Schijndel, 1994). It had already been argued that this was a mistaken interpretation of the nature of the GATT system, and the new disputes mechanism seems to make that argument less likely to be valid. A new ground for not accepting direct application, however, was suggested, that some EU legislation explicitly mentions GATT obligations; therefore, implicitly, if others are not mentioned, they do not apply. These two questionable legal challenges may reflect more an unwillingness to accept and implement the new dispute procedures than legal doubts. The worries of the two major non-compliers with GATT panels may reassure other countries wondering if the WTO panels will genuinely be stronger or more effective.

Safeguards

The pre-UR GATT agreement allowed countries whose producers were being 'seriously injured' (Article XIX) by a rise in imports to impose temporary controls on imports of that good. It did not permit these quotas to discriminate by country. Country-specific quotas were, however, among the most frequent NTBs, and making these legitimate was one of the EU's objectives for the Round. The Agreement on Safeguards will now permit this, introducing regulations on how they are used. Normally the quotas should be equal to recent shares in imports, unless the increase from 'certain members' is 'disproportionate'. Developing countries appear favoured by the provision that their imports should not be controlled unless one country accounts for more than 3% of total imports or all imports from developing countries with less than 3% account for more than 9%. But in practice, as new suppliers, they cannot avoid having 'disproportionate' increases if they are to acquire any market share. There is a four year initial and eight year total limit on all controls. Developing countries are allowed to extend this to 10 years for their own controls.

Existing controls, none of which meets the Article XIX or the new rules, must be brought into conformity with the new regulations within four years, with one exception allowed per country (only the EU has claimed this: to control Japanese cars until the end of 1999). Whether these regulations prove to represent greater discipline *de facto* will depend on whether they are more observed than the old Article XIX. They will be subject to surveillance and action under the Dispute Procedure (as were Article XIX measures). In practice, almost no Article XIX measures were taken because countries preferred illegal controls.

Anti-dumping

Anti-dumping actions became the favoured protectionist tool during the 1980s. The Tokyo Round and the unsuccessful effort to implement a 'standstill' on the use of NTBs during the Uruguay Round had brought the use of non-tariff barriers into public debate, if not into disuse. In contrast, anti-dumping actions were attractive because the GATT Code was not demanding in terms of the definitions which countries could use in determining the 'correct' price. Thus it is not difficult to find that alleged dumpers were below this, and action can be taken quickly: provisional duties can be introduced immediately. Even if the final finding is that there was no dumping, there is no compensation, only a refund of the duties (in most countries, without interest), and the goods have been obstructed at least temporarily. For perishable, fashion, or rapidly changing goods (electronic goods have been a frequent target) delay can be a sufficient obstacle. Rather than contest an anti-dumping action, therefore, some exporters chose to accept 'voluntary' restraint, which is completely outside GATT disciplines.

The principal users of anti-dumping have been the US, Australia and the EU (Table 9.1). (The record in the first half of the 1980s was similar: 1,288 investigations, 1,276 by the US, Australia, Canada and the EU (Finger and Olechowski, 1987). The US and Australia have also been the principal users of the related weapon of imposing countervailing duties (used in cases of government subsidy to an export) (Table 9.2). All had slightly different methods of finding the 'correct' price against which to judge the actual price of an import. The EU's method was considered particularly biased (Horlick, 1993 p. 5). Following a finding of dumping, and imposition of an anti-dumping duty, the duty itself is added to the costs used

Table 9.1: Initiations of anti-dumping investigations, 1985-92

	1985-86	*1986-87*	*1987-88*	*1988-89*	*1989-90*	*1990-91*	*1991-92*	*Total*
United States	65	41	30	25	24	53	62	300
Australia	55	40	21	20	23	47	76	282
European Communities	26	29	62	42	36	24	23	242
Canada	27	24	21	14	15	12	16	129
Mexico	0	2	17	17	9	14	25	84
New Zealand	0	0	4	5	1	6	13	29
Poland	0	0	0	0	0	24	0	24
Finland	0	5	5	2	0	1	0	13
Sweden	2	0	0	2	4	2	1	11
Korea, Rep.	3	1	0	0	3	2	0	9
India	0	0	0	0	0	0	5	5
Austria	0	0	0	0	0	0	4	4
Japan	0	0	0	0	0	0	3	3
Brazil	0	0	1	1	0	2	9	13
Total	178	142	161	129	115	186	237	1148
All developing	3	3	18	18	12	18	39	111
Latin America	0	2	18	18	9	16	34	97
Asia	3	1	0	0	3	2	5	14

The Anti-dumping Agreement came into force on 1 January 1980. Totals include actions regarding signatories and non-signatories to the Agreement. The reporting period covers 1 July-30 June of each year. Initiations concerning exporters of the European Communities and its member States are reported as notified. Mexico notified investigations for 1988-89 on certain products imported from the European Communities, while subsequent notifications refer to the member State of origin of the exporting firms subject to the investigation.

Sources: GATT, *Basic Instruments and Selected Documents,* 1985-92, and Annual Reports of the *European Commission to the Parliaments* 1985-91.

to compute the price,[32] thus leading to a further 'proof' of dumping unless the exporter raised his price by double the duty. The US strongly contested the EU definition (it has been one of the targets) until 1989 when in an effort to secure a permissive Uruguay Round outcome the two agreed a 'non-aggression pact' not to disagree in the negotiations.

The countries which were most often the defendants in anti-dumping actions (Table 9.3), in particular Japan and the NICs, brought to the negotiations over 100 complaints, directed at the way in which the EU and the US had used the Code. The Uruguay Round does not meet the most important complaints. The improvements include a more detailed, and thus more transparent and predictable method of determining the 'correct' price and make

---

32. As noted above, costs are explicitly excluded as an appropriate way of assessing the correct price in the pre-shipment inspection agreement.

Table 9.2: Initiations of countervailing investigations, 1985-92

	1985-86	1986-87	1987-88	1988-89	1989-90	1990-91	1991-92	Total
United States	42	11	13	9	7	7	15	104
Australia	3	3	0	2	7	10	8	33
Chile	11	0	0	0	0	2	5	18
Canada	1	4	0	1	2	0	0	8
Brazil	0	0	0	0	0	0	8	8
New Zealand	0	1	4	0	0	1	0	6
European Communities	0	0	1	2	0	0	0	3
Total	57	19	18	14	16	20	36	180
Developing	11	0	0	0	0	2	13	26

The subsidies Agreement came into force on 1 January 1980. Totals include actions regarding signatories and non-signatories to the Agreement.

Sources: GATT, *Basic Instruments and Selected Documents,* 1985-92, and Annual Reports of the *European Commission to the Parliaments* 1985-91.

provision for automatic review of a duty after five years, the 'sunset' clause.[33] The Code will be a full part of the WTO system. The Tokyo Round produced a plurilateral Code (interpreting the very general provisions under GATT Article VI) which countries could choose to accept or not. But the new rules effectively follow those of the EU,[34] and the five year review can extend the duty (Horlick, 1993). The duties can be contested under the Disputes procedure only on objections to the methods and the factual findings. As noted in Chapter 5, clothing and textiles can now be the subject of anti-dumping investigations. A further extension goes some way towards meeting the EU complaints about circumvention and that it had to take action against each firm when a large number of suppliers were alleged to be dumping the same product. The new version introduces the concept of cumulative effects on the domestic industry and permits a country to take action, without further investigation, against parts sent for assembly of an item already subject to duty or from the same company in another supplying country (Horlick, 1993). The EU's request to be allowed to extend duties to other firms in the same country exporting the same products, however, was not adopted. In addition to the changes resulting from the Uruguay Round, imposition of EU anti-dumping and countervailing duties has been made easier by a simultaneous EU decision that in future action can be taken by simple majority in the Council of Ministers, no longer requiring a qualified majority.

33. GATT also gives considerable weight to the inclusion of a *de minimis* clause, banning anti-dumping duties of under 2% (cf. GATT 1993 *developing*). It is difficult to see this as a great advance, except perhaps in removing nuisance duties; many countries already applied a similar cut-off. Nuisance investigations, even without imposition of a duty, have been more of a burden than nuisance duties.

34. In the words of the EU's own appraisal of the negotiations, 'This will mean that EC importers face the same regime as before but that exporters can now benefit from the experience and insights that the Community has in running its AD policy' (EU, 1994 *Uruguay Round*, p. 20)

98

Table 9.3 Exporters subject to anti-dumping investigations, 1985-92

Asia		Latin America		Africa	
Korea	78	Brazil	54	S. Africa	6
China	69	Mexico	22	Egypt	3
Chinese Taipei	68	Argentina	17	Kenya	1
Hong Kong	22	Venezuela	14	Libya	1
Thailand	19	Colombia	5	Zimbabwe	1
Singapore	18	Chile	3	Tunisia	1
India	17	Trinidad and Tobago	2		
Malaysia	12	Costa Rica	1		
Indonesia	9	Ecuador	1		
Israel	8	El Salvador	1		
Philippines	5	Peru	1		
Bangladesh	3	Uruguay	1		
Macau	1				
Pakistan	1				
Papua New Guinea	1				
Sub-Totals	338		122		13
Developing	473				
Total	**1148**				

The reporting period covers 1 July 1985 to 30 June 1992. Initiations concerning exporters of the European Communities and its member States are reported as notified. Mexico notified investigations for 1988-89 on certain products imported from the European Communities, while subsequent notifications refer to the member State of origin of the exporting firms subject to the investigation.

Sources: GATT, *Basic Instruments and Selected Documents,* 1985-92, and Annual Reports of the *European Commission to the Parliaments* 1985-91.

The anti-dumping rules make no distinction in their application between developed and developing countries (unless the minor reduction in the calculated 'correct' price for new producers is more often used by the developing); the new rules on countervailing duties (against domestic subsidies to production or export) do have higher *de minimis* provisions for them and some exemption for subsidies, partly to bring them into line with the more relaxed rules on subsidies and longer periods of adjustment allowed to developing countries by the other sections of the Settlement. The only special mention of developing countries in the anti-dumping provisions is that they may need assistance to meet the more detailed provisions when taking their own anti-dumping actions. This is a new development (Table 9.1), but a rapidly increasing one. Mexico has been the leader (and has started to apply an EU-type cost definition), and both Mexico and Brazil have had actions ruled unacceptable because of failure to follow procedure. Other developing countries are also starting to act or at least reforming their national legislation to increase their power to do so (including some ASEAN countries, South Africa), but it is notable that in general the Asian countries which have been the principal targets (Tables 9.3 and 9.4) have not been among the leaders in taking action (Tables 9.1 and 9.2).

The appearance of developing countries on both sides of anti-dumping and countervailing actions makes it more difficult than it might have seemed at the beginning of the Uruguay Round to assess the nature of the settlement's effect on them. They are still disproportionately more targets than actors. They took only about 10% of the anti-dumping actions over the period of the Round, rising to a sixth in the most recent year for which data are published, while they were the subject of 40% of the investigations (they had been the target of 39% of US actions in the previous five years; in that period actions against Latin America and Asia had been almost equal). The numbers are slightly higher for countervailing actions, but with the same disproportion. The Asian countries in particular have suffered from anti-dumping actions, and if actions now occur in clothing, China and Korea (already the two developing countries with most investigations) are likely to be targets. The increased trade among the Asian countries may also lead to actions among themselves.

As developing country producers may compete more on cost factors than those in industrial countries, the increased scope of the anti-dumping actions is more likely to damage them than industrial countries. This is reinforced by the increased respectability given to this form of protection by its greater prominence in the WTO system and by such innovations as GATT courses in how to take anti-dumping action for developing countries. This also increases the uncertainty of the system of trade regulation by introducing difficult, if not arbitrary, calculations (the costs and profits) and by explicitly accepting uncertain and bargaining criteria (the representations of users of the imports and the concept of damage to a local industry). Anti-dumping may also be the only part of the system in which individual firms, rather than governments, are accepted as the basic actors, both as initiators of actions and as their targets. In other areas, it is assumed that governments are responsible for actions affecting trade (even if national regulations delegate this function to other organisations, as was noted for services in Chapter 7). The anti-dumping agreement does not, however, increase certainty for individual firms, because the impact on target firms depends on whether a competing firm in the importing country chooses to take action, and both firms depend on the decisions of their governments on whether to take a disputed result to the dispute settlement procedure. If uncertainty is believed to damage small and inexperienced countries more than others, this is another form of discrimination against the developing countries.

Both the anti-dumping procedures and the subsidies codes (on which countervailing actions would be based) are now subject to much more precise regulation. In itself, this increases certainty and reduces the possibility of arbitrary action, but it also makes any dispute potentially more technically complicated (or 'lawyer intensive': Agosin, et al., p. 15). This could put poor or inexperienced countries and new firms at a disadvantage. The response offered by GATT (and other international institutions) is increased training.

Table 9.4: Exporters subject to countervailing investigations, 1985-92

Asia		Latin America		Africa	
Thailand	9	Brazil	17	Kenya	1
Malaysia	7	Argentina	6	Zimbabwe	1
Chinese Taipei	6	Venezuela	6		
China	5	Mexico	5		
Israel	5	Peru	3		
Singapore	5	Colombia	2		
India	4	Chile	1		
Korea	4	Costa Rica	1		
Bangladesh	1	Ecuador	1		
Pakistan	1	El Salvador	1		
		Uruguay	1		
Sub-Totals	47		44		2
Developing	93				
Total	180				

The Subsidies Agreement came into force on 1 January 1980. All totals include actions regarding signatories and non-signatories to the Agreement.

Sources: GATT, *Basic Instruments and Selected Documents,* 1985-92, and Annual Reports of the *European Commission to the Parliaments* 1985-91.

Previous Rounds which have gradually restricted the traditional forms of protection, tariffs, then NTBs, then subsidies . . . have usually been followed by successful searches for new forms of protection. It is, however, more unusual for these to be built into the settlement as they have been for safeguards and anti-dumping. It is perhaps not surprising that US importers have opposed the extension of US legislation to take advantage of the new methods of calculation (and even exporters have considered that these could bring greater risks of retaliatory action). The normal 'practical' argument, that if the system does not propose a regulated means, unregulated investigations will be used, does not seem to apply as Mexico has continued to complain that the US is misapplying the rules.

10. The World Trading Organisation

Formally, the reason for differentiating the future organisation from the present GATT is that it needs to cover the new areas, which are not explicitly under GATT.[35] It is now argued that these issues are so different in kind, because they influence investment and national regulation, that they cannot be brought under the old GATT. This is of course the reverse of the argument for including them in the Uruguay Round in the first place, that they were so closely related to trade that they had now to be included in the same negotiations. It was those countries which opposed the inclusion of services at the beginning of the Uruguay Round which insisted that the negotiation and eventual settlement be kept separate from the existing areas of competence of GATT. These countries, as we have seen, accepted and joined in the services agreement in the final settlement and, in areas like Dispute Settlement, they have accepted them implicitly as full parts of the procedures (the provision for retaliatory action across Agreements). This removes the original reason for the WTO; new subjects have been brought into GATT in the past.

There remain three reasons for the WTO. The intention is to encourage, if not actually compel, countries to accept all the new areas, rather than leaving them as side agreements, called by GATT 'plurilateral agreements', as was done for some issues after the Tokyo Round. (In principle, GATT remains in existence for those who do not join the WTO, but in contrast to the past the presumption will be that countries join or opt out, rather than that they opt in.)[36] Some plurilateral agreements do remain: government procurement and effectively all services except the framework itself, so that clearly this is not a sufficient explanation. Second, there is a desire to be seen to be strengthening the basis of the international trade system, not just more comprehensive coverage, but clear obligations and better enforceability, and raising the formal status of the organisation is a part of this.[37] Third, the new organisation will be more overtly part of the international policy system, not simply an administrative body, with a Ministerial Conference every two years, rather than only when needed to start or end a negotiating Round.[38] There is here an element of inter-organisational rivalry, with one of the functions of the WTO being defined as 'to cooperate, as appropriate, with the International Monetary Fund, the International Bank for Reconstruction and Development and its affiliated agencies' (GATT, 1993 *developing* p. 30). Such co-operation among international agencies is supposed to be the norm. Its explicit inclusion here, the proposal to coordinate WTO and IMF country studies, and a more specific suggestion of a permanent council at summit and ministerial level to deal jointly with policy affecting all three of the WTO, IMF,

---

35. 'The agreements on goods, services and intellectual property protection are the three pillars of the WTO' (Sutherland, 1994, 30 May speech).

36. The US may leave GATT formally when it adheres to the WTO, creating doubt about its obligations to any countries which did not ratify the WTO, and about theirs to it. So far (December 1994) no other country had plans to do the same or to remain permanently in GATT rather than WTO.

37. 'The agreement to establish the WTO not only provides a major *institutional* boost to the multilateral trading system, but also a fundamental reform of the dispute settlement system.' (Sutherland, 1994, 16 June) (emphasis in original).

38. 'Beyond these administrative functions, [the WTO] will raise the political profile of trade - a profile which has already been lifted greatly by the Uruguay Round. The WTO will have regular - instead of occasional - direct Ministerial involvement. It will have a clear mandate to act as a forum for further trade negotiations.' (Sutherland, 1994, January 28).

three of the WTO, IMF, and World Bank (Sutherland 1994, January 28), appear to be an attempt to push the organisation forward as more than the powerless secretariat which it has always claimed to be in the past.

The basic objective is to establish a framework and a forum for future trade and other international economic negotiations. There are demands on the international trading system which GATT has not met in the past. Comprehensive coverage of trade in goods and greater regulatory power have been attempted in the Uruguay Round settlement, even if it remains to be seen how effective these will be. The framework and some regulation have been built for coverage of services and the trade-related areas. There is an implicit assumption in areas like TRIPs, but also in the negotiations on services (in particular the working groups on professional standards), that recognition or harmonisation of international standards is an appropriate area for GATT action. This pushes it very much in the direction which has led to increasing international intervention within the EU. But there is also an extension in the role of trade negotiations as a continuing process. The long Tokyo Round and the much longer Uruguay Round have made many countries and traders question the concept of periodic Rounds and support a more permanent system for negotiations. The provisions made in the settlement for some areas to start further negotiations immediately and others to do so within a set interval (five years for agriculture and services, for example) go part of the way in this direction. It is possible that the regular ministerial meetings will permit the identification of new problems or opportunities for negotiations on a more regular basis. An obstacle to continuing negotiations which has been raised in the past is that in many cases concessions in one sector must be bargained against those in another. Therefore, in order to accommodate all the interests of all the countries, all sectors must be on the table simultaneously. The explicit provision of cross-retaliation in the Dispute Settlement procedure, the insistence on including most of the new areas in the WTO, not as optional plurilateral agreements, and the implicit recognition of the tariff cuts which had been made by some developing countries during, but outside, the negotiations as acceptable 'credits' against concessions demanded from them during the Round, all provide potential models of methods for managing partial negotiations outside fully comprehensive Rounds.

Such partial negotiations would make it possible for developing countries to form *ad hoc* negotiating groups on particular issues, as the textile and clothing exporters and the food importers did during the Uruguay Round. The old model of all developing countries as a single group disappeared early in the Round.

A problem which has already arisen for developing countries, and for GATT or the WTO as an institution in trade policy for goods, and which will become increasingly important as new issues are brought into the WTO system, is how to reconcile the view that opening trade is beneficial with the format of negotiations which set exporters, assumed to want to gain access, against importers, assumed to want to avoid 'conceding' access. In some issues, there are no clear lines drawn for country-against-country talks. Services and TRIPs, among the new issues, are clearly about the desirable level of regulation in general, as well as the effects of one country on another, not only about market access. It is certain that regulatory issues in competition policy will be brought into question, through questioning countries' procedures using existing WTO rules or as new issues. If the environment or social issues like labour standards come into play in the future, regulation rather than access will be even more the issue. The role of access in these is more as a reason for international concern or an enforcement mechanism than as the central question.

For developing countries, the new prominence of these issues has the effect of making the powers given or denied to the WTO more important relative to the negotiating strength of its trading partners. In some cases it opens up the possibility of new alliances across the developing-industrial country division. This and the fact that the WTO has maintained the GATT structure of a single tier, one-country one-vote Council, could encourage their participation in the WTO and in the international trading system. Under the GATT, the absence of a firm institutional basis tended to give 'consensus' *de facto* a major role. The WTO has explicit provisions for how decisions are made in the absence of consensus, usually a demanding requirement of three quarters (Jackson, 1994). [39]

What remains missing is provision for the type of institutional initiative which the IMF and the World Bank (and other parts of the UN system) have long considered a normal part of their responsibilities. The obstacle is not simply that on some questions (starting an investigation under the disputes procedure, for example) the initial complaint must come from outside. There appears to remain an organisational unwillingness to raise new questions, rather than responding to them. On the other hand, GATT has been increasingly willing to act on already identified problems. The formal involvement of the Secretariat in identifying and presenting all agreed and all outstanding questions during the Round in the form of the 'Dunkel Draft' of the final settlement; its reorganisation of the negotiations when the initial structure had stalled; the switch to a more critical use of the Trade Policy Reviews; the very active part played by Peter Sutherland as Director-General in insisting on the benefits of reaching agreement at the end of the Round; none of these would have been seen in the 1970s, and further moves in the direction of setting the agenda are therefore likely.

The new issues and the increasing importance of questions about how and how much governments regulate economic activities are also making anomalous the exclusion of any way of taking account of any interests other than those of the governments: interests may differ within countries and some may link groups across countries. As long as GATT's principal function was seen as providing a framework of rules for governments' intervention in external trade (regulation of tariffs and NTBs) and for ensuring equal treatment of all countries at this level (MFN treatment), its constituency was clearly governments. If the WTO is dealing with the actions of firms and their effect on producers and importers in another country (anti-dumping, preshipment inspection), with the role of governments in assisting and regulating their own firms and consumers (subsidies, services regulation, TRIPs), and potentially with the presence or absence of regulations on the environment or labour standards, then it is not only governments which have an interest. If it is to have an institutional commitment to liberalising trade, parallel with the type of official views on how to deal with capital flows, exchange rates, and managing the economy observed in the IMF or the World Bank, then governments cease to be its appropriate constituency: it is the

---

39. Most issues have been and are expected to be decided by consensus (although if permanent negotiations or the more effective dispute settlement procedure bring more controversy this could change). Changes or waivers in the basic Agreement will require three quarters (formerly two thirds) of all members for the most important articles, out of a membership of 124, with 18 new countries' applications under consideration. (The EU has been accepted as a member in its own right, along with Member states, but the total number of votes is expressly limited to the total number of its member states.)

104

purchasers of goods and services, companies or consumers, for which economic theory argues that free trade is a benefit, not (at least not necessarily) national states.

There is a demand for such participation, by industrial, consumer, environmental and other interest groups.[40] Consumers are recognised by the anti-dumping settlement as having a role at national level. The industrial interests concerned are not only the traditional multinational companies, which have an indirect role through their acceptance as lobbyists within the trade structures of individual countries, but an increasing number of smaller companies trading and investing as part of their normal operations, as the reduction of international barriers makes international trade look less exotic and more a matter of everyday economic activity. Asia is an area where this is particularly important. The increased importance of all these cross-border contacts has helped to encourage the awareness of services and intellectual property as important in international competitiveness.

The 1994 controversies in both the US and EU over how far legislatures should have a voice in ratifying and supervising the UR Agreement or modifying or controlling future negotiations will give strength to these pressures.[41] The agreement for setting up the WTO does include provision that 'the Council may make appropriate arrangements for consultation and cooperation with non-government organizations concerned with matters related to those of the WTO' (Article V, 2), but this has not received the same emphasis in GATT press releases or speeches as Article V, 1, on co-operation with other intergovernment organisations.

The two new issues for future negotiations which have already been raised have important implications for the developing countries. The environment was accepted at the signing of the Uruguay Round Settlement in April 1994 as part of the agenda for the WTO; social standards have not yet been formally included, but with both the EU Trade Commissioner and the US President supporting their inclusion, they are likely to be adopted. It is too early to consider these in detail, and this goes well beyond the impact of the Uruguay Round except in two elements.

1. The inclusion of new issues in this Round which have only a tenuous justification as 'trade-related' has clearly opened the way for questions which in the past only outside pressure groups, not any of the major governments, wanted to bring into GATT.

2. Secondly, the precedent that each Round has encouraged new forms of protection, by barring or limiting some of the old, suggests that the new issues may be appearing with the protection of producers, rather than of the environment or labour in mind.

For both, there is the precedent that they have been added to international agreements; the NAFTA agreement among the US, Canada and Mexico as well as the EU. The first complaint under the labour law agreement of NAFTA was made by the US against a Japanese investor (Sony) in Mexico. That it was not against either a Mexican company or a US investor may

40. The International Organisation of Consumers Unions and the UK National Consumer Council have supported representation in the WTO (IOCU, 1994; NCC, 1994).

41. The question also arose in the House of Commons debate on the Round, with demands for the WTO to be 'a proper and democratic organisation' (House of Commons, Hansard, 1994 col. 591).

suggest motives other than concern for union rights. As discussed in Chapter 2, labour rights have also been part of US preferential arrangements. Both issues have already affected other international institutions. The World Bank includes environmental assessments in its project assessments and 1994 US legislation would require the Bank to include labour standards as a condition in its lending.

The developing countries, as a group, have opposed including these issues on the grounds that they are protectionist in intent. There has been strong opposition from the ASEAN countries. Eventually, as in services, they will probably nuance and differentiate their opposition, and (again as in services) the issues offer some opportunities for developing countries to make demands. It is not only or even mainly developing countries which pollute or damage the environment. Labour standards in some industrial countries do not meet the minimum ILO standards, with less justification on the grounds of poverty or inexperience. South Africa is already considering its position, with competition from lower-wage countries in Africa and Asia probably supplementing the motive of extending the new government's historical interest in human rights. There remains, however, the institutional issue of whether an organisation whose structure and objectives are based on trade issues is the most suitable forum for analysing or taking action on all 'trade-related' questions, especially where other international organisations exist, for example, the International Labour Organisation. Strengthening them could be an alternative approach.

11. Conclusions and summary

The quantifiable effects which we have found and summarised in Chapter 6 are on average positive, but insignificant in size and for some sectors and groups uncertain in sign.[42] The services agreements (Chapter 7) are probably on balance positive for developing countries as a group; those on TRIPs, TRIMs, etc. discussed in Chapter 8, small and uncertain. They gain on dispute settlement, and from increased information from the Trade Policy Reviews, but probably lose on the new PSI safeguard and anti-dumping rules. A stronger more prominent WTO should be a gain. Some conclusions about the direction and the nature of the effects, however, are firmly based. The final conclusion from these remains as suggested in Chapter 1: the gains come mainly from the reforms, extension, and reinforcement of an orderly rule-based system of international economic relations. Their significance for developing countries derives from these countries' growing exposure to that system, and their relative weakness in a less orderly system. Calculating the final signs and the distribution of benefits is impossible by these methods, but the traditional tool of revealed preference, in this case countries' own statements and their ratifications of the agreement, suggests that most countries see the results as positive, even among the poorest for whom the calculated effects are negative. The demands are for the principle of enhanced assistance to be extended from food imports to all the costs of their reforms, but with more emphasis on the technical and administrative costs than on food import costs or preference erosion (UN Economic Commission for Africa, 1994; UN Economic Commision for Asia, 1994).

Since 1991, a number of estimates of the effect of the Uruguay Round in total and on developing countries have been published by international organisations and by other groups. It remains true, however, that these have not been made in the context, or by the methods of the normal round of forecasting or other general macroeconomic models and until the end of the Round in 1993 most were published in the context of a strong advocacy of international collaboration in general and a successful Uruguay Round in particular. This advocacy does not fit the conventional international trade theory or the assumption which has guided much official advice to developing countries in the last 15 years, that the principal benefits (except under certain assumptions about imperfect markets and market power) of liberalising trade accrue to the liberalising country. Its gains from others' liberalisation and, hence, perhaps, from using its liberalisation as a bargaining tool to encourage general liberalisation are secondary.

Such estimates have also excluded (as has this report) quantitative assessments of the impact of the services agreement and (in most cases) of the general confidence effects either of reaching any agreement or of reducing the inherent uncertainty in trade by increasing the regulatory strength of GATT/WTO. For these reasons, there has been a tendency to argue that they underestimate the benefits to all countries and to the developing countries (as weak bargainers) in particular. There has also been an argument that comparing the outcome simply to the actual or pre-Round position is an underestimate because without the Round things would have got worse, and would continue to do so. The prospect, then the fact, of an agreement were themselves restraining influences on the protection that would otherwise have been observed. This report has in several cases argued the reverse, that some parts of the agreement would have been implemented without the Round, perhaps in different terms or

---

42. For comparison with other estimates, it can be noted that the 1% increase in exports reported in Chapter 6 is equal to US $10-15 billion.

with a different timetable, because of existing tendencies to remove the barriers. The sectors where this argument was used included temperate agriculture (both the EU and US supports were already under review and reform); the reductions in tariffs and NTBs by the Asian NICs and the major Latin American countries; the reform, if not the abolition, of the MFA; some of the initiatives on services; the spread of intellectual protection; and agreements on investment and preshipment inspection. We have also argued, however, that some reduction of preference margins and, more broadly, of differential treatment of the developing countries was occurring outside the Round; therefore that the negative as well as the positive effects of the Round may be overestimated.

In almost all the sectors, quantified and unquantified, it is the more advanced Asian countries which appear to gain most, or to have most chance of gaining and least to lose. The goods which they trade include those in which there are major reforms; they have less to lose in preferences; and they are moving into the activities and concerns which were the motives behind the industrial countries' choice of the new areas to include. The Latin American countries have already liberalised their own trade, their services are less concentrated in regulated sectors, and they are less advanced in some of the other areas. But they gain geographically, because of the reforms in temperate agriculture; on some tariffs; and, because of others' loss of preferential margin, in tropical agriculture. India, possibly Pakistan, probably not Bangladesh and Sri Lanka, gain enough on the MFA reforms to do well on balance, and India at least is moving into some of the other manufactures and services which offer prospects for gains. The Caribbean and some of the other smaller countries face more mixed prospects, with apparent losses on present exports, but histories of moving rapidly from one export to another as conditions change.

The area which has none of these advantages is Africa. This is not surprising if we return to the arguments for expecting the developing countries to do well out of participating in this Round. Africa does not yet have the greater involvement in trade observed for the average of developing countries. It does not have increased bargaining power because of higher imports from the industrial countries. It is not able to attract investment and associated technology. It has not yet suffered from complaints in disputes or anti-dumping investigations. It does not export products affected by the highest trade barriers and has not yet faced protectionist action by the industrial countries. Its preferences have given it access equal to or beyond what other countries are now gaining, so it can only lose from the levelling up of others. It may benefit from the general regulation and market opening in the future, and it has the possibility of gain from the subsidies to food importers (if these become reality) or from the WTO's new unit to look after the least developed countries and assist them to use their new opportunities.

Even for the countries which may gain from the Round, the examination in Chapter 6 of the staging of the agreements suggests that the gains will be slow to appear and could be preceded by periods of loss.

The commitment of all the governments in the Round and of the other major international institutions to achieving a settlement by the end of the negotiations was impressive. The effect on confidence of the implication that they will not try to frustrate the agreements reached cannot be negative. The only negative marks here were on anti-dumping (and, prospectively, on the new issues of the environment and labour conditions, but these could not have effects

108

for several years). Past experience suggests that other forms of protection may also emerge, but there is no evidence that the settlement will have increased this probability, and the inclusion of some of the areas which have been used for this purpose since the last Round (services, intellectual property) may give a temporary respite while the new loopholes are found.

The effects of the agriculture and MFA agreements will be clearly positive for the most efficient producers, and positive for all developing countries in their signal that in future markets will be determined more by competitiveness and less by quotas, but at a short-term cost, possibly, in agriculture and, probably, in clothing, for some countries which have benefited from the protection. In both cases, however, the countries concerned have themselves accepted these losses as compensated either by other elements of the Agreement or as inevitable with or without it.[43]

The idea of general, but unspecific, preferences in all areas of the GATT for all developing countries has disappeared. Specific elements of special treatment have been substituted, in obligations or periods of adjustment, in some sections of the Agreement, and there is now a clear differentiation between 'developing', i.e. middle-income developing, and 'least developed'. This provides a stronger, because statutory, entitlement where it is given, but its use as a complete substitute for the general commitment has risks. The presumption in the time-limited concessions that countries can reach 'developed' maturity within a predictable (and quite short in historical terms) period is inconsistent with past experience, of varying paths and reversals. It imposes international restrictions on countries' policies earlier in their development than other countries have accepted in the past. Bound tariffs, intellectual property and services are the obvious examples, but the regulations on subsidies and government intervention in other sectors offer others. Economic theory and the current preferences of the developing countries' present governments argue that these restrictions only prevent undesirable policies; other regimes with different development strategies have not accepted these arguments in the past. Binding has removed the possibility of a reversion to these policies. The specific issue of how to find a substitute for the well-documented benefit of preferences or other trade interventions at the point of entry of a product, company, or country into a new market has not been dealt with (except for a limited temporary allowance on pricing under the anti-dumping agreement).

The question of whether there should be compensation for developing (or other) countries which lose advantages which they have enjoyed because of other countries' protectionist policies when these policies are reformed has produced a very unsatisfactory solution. In the past, the answer was no. The only provisions for compensation were for countries shown to be damaged either by a policy condemned by a panel under the dispute settlement provisions or by a regional trading group judged to be trade-diverting. The calculations might be difficult or controversial, but the principle was clear. This Round has introduced the possibility (not backed by financial resources) of compensation for one form of damage only, the loss of low-cost food imports. Chapters 3 and 6 have suggested that the effects of this will be small, uncertain, and probably not as great as the potential effects of other reforms. The introduction

43. It is UNCTAD, some regional organisations and non-official governmental groups which have expressed most concern about the outcome.

of areas like TRIPs has brought in other new criteria, notably the right to payment for intellectual property. Whatever the merits of these criteria, they take trade negotiations into new areas of regulation rather than access to markets.

The definition of 'developing countries' has been left open, and that for 'least developed' tied to a UN definition designed for other purposes. Both cut across the definitions used by other international agencies and bilaterally by countries offering preferential trade arrangements. With clear differences in obligations tied to the definitions, it will rapidly become necessary to find a formal criterion for defining these countries, and a means of amending the definitions when this is needed in the future.

In assessing the long-term impact of the WTO, it is necessary to predict how it will adapt to an increasingly integrated world economy. Two changes have been suggested here. The first is the growing importance of non-trade questions (in the immediate future, the environment and labour conditions). The second is the increasing role of actors other than governments on the international scene.

GATT, with the support of its members, has proved, both in the new areas brought into the Uruguay Round and in its acceptance of the environment as a new issue, more than eager to extend its competence to subjects increasingly tenuously related to trade. This report has suggested that its traditional attitudes and methods may need adapting more than it has yet realised to deal appropriately with these. In contrast, it remains very reluctant to deal directly with interests outside governments. It is enthusiastic about the possibility of co-operation with two of the traditional major international institutions, the IMF and World Bank (these have yet to show reciprocal enthusiasm), but it has shown little interest in co-operating with others. On TRIPs, it accepts the Conventions evolved by others, but expects its own rulings to override those of WIPO, the existing World Intellectual Property Organisation. The 'new issues' will raise the question of overlap with the responsibilities of the ILO. Unlike the IMF and World Bank, it does not consider itself even formally part of the UN system. As more non-trade issues come to be seen as 'trade-related' and, correspondingly, more trade issues are 'related' to investment, labour, industrial and agricultural policy, and development, relations with other agencies, allocating responsibilities among them, and the accountability of all of them for their policies to governments and others will become significant questions. Except for permitting the membership of the EU, it has shown less interest in regional organisations. The settlement reduces their economic attractions (lowering MFN barriers lowers the potential for preferential arrangements), and makes the formal conditions for them more rigorous. If NAFTA, Lomé, and other organisations within Latin America, Africa, and Asia, and between different areas become increasingly important, and more move beyond purely trade areas into other economic and political co-operation, the approach of simply regulating their progress towards free trade will become inadequate. Like the EU, they will have international interests and responsibilities which affect the rest of the world.

The settlement has benefited all the countries with reasonable current prospects for benefiting from trade. It has more than met most of its 1986 objectives, and it meets the most rigorous economic test, of being accepted by the participants (at least by the developing countries; the ratification doubts were found among the industrial). Settling one set of questions has, as in all previous Rounds, brought forward the next set.

Appendix 1

Central and Eastern Europe (CEC) and the Former Soviet Union (FSU)

In terms of economic impact on the 'economies in transition', the agreement is overshadowed – and complicated – by the signing of the Europe Agreements between Poland, the Czech and Slovak Republics, Hungary, Romania and Bulgaria – severally – and the Economic Union and the Partnership and Cooperation Agreements between Russia and the Ukraine, and in due course other FSU republics, with the EU. These, in particular the Europe Agreements, give the transition economies a considerable degree of preferential access to the EU market. Their preferences are second only to those of the ACP states. And, like those of the ACP, their new preferential margins will be eroded by reductions in MFN tariff rates. In this section we only aim to draw attention to certain effects of the UR agreement on the developing countries which will come about through changes in their access to markets in the CEC and the FSU, and changes in their competitive position vis-à-vis these countries in third markets.

Under the former socialist regimes, the CEC-FSU countries were constrained in their trading relationships by an autarky, partly self-imposed, partly the result of western policies, and a bias towards import substitution. A division of labour among the various FSU republics and their CEC partners was established, with different countries within the bloc allocated responsibility for the production of different groups of products, based only to a minor extent on comparative advantage (except where natural resources dictated it). Price signals were distorted by many factors including artificial exchange rates, often differentiated by product, but even then they were second to political preferences in favour of developing complementarities within the CMEA bloc. In the early years trade with the West was discouraged for ideological reasons, though the need for Western capital goods to supplement their technologically inferior products led to increasing links through the 1970s and 1980s and the active promotion of exports to the West. Even then East-West trade was hampered by lack of capacity to adapt to the needs or preferences of western markets.

Now with the institutional constraints lifted, functioning foreign exchange markets or even currencies convertible for trade purposes and sourcing decisions based on economic criteria, trade with the west, particularly among the CEC is expanding rapidly. Table A1 shows the surge in exports of manufactures from the CEC to the EU in 1991 and 1992. A number of studies (Collins and Rodrik, 1991, Hamilton and Winters, 1992, and Stern *et al.*, 1992) predict continued, rapid increases, assisted to a limited extent by preferential treatment in EU markets, and to a lesser extent through the GSP of other western countries. Stern *et al.* for example, estimate that those trade flows will grow at some 1½ times the growth in world trade as a whole with the Hamilton-Winters results giving similar relative orders of magnitude and country rankings for potential trade expansion.

To judge the potential competitive threat of CEC and FSU exports to those of the developing countries we need a plausible sectoral breakdown of those exports. In summary, Collins and Rodrik conclude that the FSU will basically export energy and raw materials, while the CEC will export agricultural goods, processed food and a wide range of manufactured products. Stern *et al.*'s projections of CEC-FSU exports of manufactures give a plausible if perhaps rather too dramatic picture; the intention was to give the upper bound of

Table A1: Merchandise exports of Central and Eastern Europe and the Former Soviet Union to the EU by product, 1990-92, $ billion

	year	Bulgaria	fmr. Czechoslovakia	Hungary	Poland	Romania	fmr. USSR
Total	1990	1084	4453	4563	7745	2221	25379
merchandise	1991	927	5040	4582	7712	1822	21633
	1992	1166	7177	5263	9238	1861	22005
Primary	1990	354	941	1470	3212	565	19184
Products	1991	356	955	1574	3137	403	16087
	1992	403	1192	1516	3335	205	16389
Manufactures	1990	712	3418	3016	4210	1642	4723
	1991	557	3994	2952	4507	1401	3401
	1992	755	5843	3678	5806	1638	3838
Food	1990	221	281	965	1416	52	281
	1991	224	301	1106	1306	88	367
	1992	220	346	1041	1196	91	506
Raw materials	1990	36	301	173	295	39	1860
	1991	49	219	207	294	33	1294
	1992	62	274	206	407	41	1362
Ores and	1990	18	85	87	236	5	329
minerals	1991	32	167	73	310	17	251
	1992	44	236	88	386	9	586
Fuels	1990	55	244	108	794	415	15311
	1991	23	206	107	698	233	12687
	1992	20	221	84	669	53	
							12694
Non-ferrous	1990	24	29	136	471	55	1404
metals	1991	84	119	82	529	31	1487
	1992	58	114	97	678	11	1690
Iron and steel	1990	98	497	210	374	119	1061
	1991	76	501	148	341	84	548
	1992	69	717	173	420	131	685
Chemicals	1990	94	490	399	640	75	987
	1991	100	569	447	693	92	901
	1992	96	630	518	658	91	1217
Other semi-	1990	53	513	351	667	188	700
manufactures	1991	53	742	402	879	174	636
	1992	78	1245	482	1189	171	683
Machinery	1990	310	1117	12948	1191	327	1677
and transport	1991	123	1048	774	851	176	1075
equipment	1992	141	1487	1007	1238	155	945
Textiles	1990	27	238	134	142	45	80
	1991	26	288	128	146	38	72
	1992	46	371	131	171	40	78
Clothing	1990	75	188	483	673	454	8
	1991	114	347	584	953	438	26
	1992	205	541	764	1296	618	113
Other	1990	56	376	391	539	433	231
consumer	1991	104	400	468	661	409	164
goods	1992	121	854	603	838	440	165

Source: GATT, *International Trade Statistics*, 1993, GATT, Geneva.

a probability range. The annual average growth rates of CEC-FSU manufactured exports to the EU are projected at 14.0% for the period 1988 to 1995 and 10.7% for 1995 to 2010.

Prior to 1989 CEC-FSU manufactured exports to the EC were heavily concentrated in a few industries – clothing with footwear and leather goods (15% in 1987), timber and furniture (15%), ferrous and non-ferrous metals (14%), chemicals including artificial fibres (11%), food, drink and tobacco (9%). Stern *et al.* foresee a diversification of CEC-FSU manufactured exports. The projected growth rates in the 'traditional' export industries, textiles, clothing and footwear and ferrous and non-ferrous metals, are below those of the new export industries, primarily in engineering. The exception is chemicals which will be the most important export industry for the CEC-FSU as a whole in 2010, accounting for 14% of manufactured exports to the EU. Metals are projected to increase their share marginally up to 1995 up to 15%) and then fall back sharply to only 8% in 2005. Clothing and footwear was the most important export industry in 1987. In 1995 it will be the fourth most important with a projected 13 percent of manufacturing exports. In 2010 it will not feature in the top 6 for any CEC or FSU country.

Support for the Stern *et al.* results is provided by the Hamilton and Winters (1992) argument that the high level of educational attainment in CEC-FSU countries gives them a comparative advantage in 'hi-tech' and 'mid-tech' goods. This advantage would favour competitiveness in engineering products and transport goods at the expense of metals and minerals, chemicals, food, drink and tobacco, textiles and clothing, footwear and leather goods.

In moving to a more sophisticated mix of exports, the CEC would be reverting to an earlier pattern of trade. In 1981 engineering goods were more important than metals, chemicals or light industry (including clothing and footwear) in Poland's exports, both within the CMEA and beyond (see Chavigny, 1992). To the extent that they are unable to meet the higher quality requirements of the developed economies, the CEC will have to search for markets among the developing countries.

In the short run protectionist pressures in the EU and elsewhere among the developed countries will also push in the same directions. In the longer term, however, it seems appropriate to assume that each of the CEC either joins the EU or enters a free trade area with it; indeed the fact that the comparative advantages of these countries could develop beyond their current major export sectors will speed up the process of accession to the EU or the establishment of FTAs.

These developments in East-West trade are in the main the result of changes in the political and economic structures in the CEC and FSU economies, together with some modest help in the form of improved access to western markets. They are not to any large extent affected by the Uruguay Round agreement, though they may be marginally circumscribed by the reduction in the value of EU special, and non-EU GSP, preferences. Competition in the export markets of the developing countries will be largely concentrated in manufactures, so it will be the NICs and the newly emerging exporters of manufactures in South East Asia and Latin America that will be most affected. Exports of ores and minerals and precious metals – which in most cases enter the industrialised markets without tariff or other barriers – will have depressing effects on the world prices of these products in the short to medium term. In the longer term as output in the CEC and FSU expands, demand for these products will also increase and ultimately the effect of the breakdown of the eastern command economies may be stronger world prices than would otherwise have obtained.

In two sectors, however, the agreement could be important for East-South competition on third markets: agriculture and clothing and textiles. In agricultural goods, the CEC countries remain subject to CAP regulations where applicable. This implies that they could make gains from the liberalisation of temperate agricultural products which would mean some erosion of the EU preferences for the developing countries. The ACP preferences on cut flowers, soft fruits and some vegetables coming from certain African countries, in particular Kenya, will be eroded, as will the GSP preferences on the same goods from Latin America. Although the CEC products are not usually identical to those from the warmer developing countries, they are often close enough to be substitutes. In the short term the impact of the European Agreements on developing country exports will be limited to a few, not critical, sectors.

114

Appendix 2: Commitments on Services

Table A2: Commitments on services with sector-specific limitations
(Share of bound service activities)

Region	Cross-border			Consumption abroad			Commercial presence			Natural persons		
	No limits	Limits	Unbound	No limits	Limits	Unbound	No limits	Limits	Unbound	No limits	Limits	Unbound
North America	78	16	6	83	11	6	67	32	2	82	17	1
Latin America	50	3	47	63	0	34	70	21	9	81	6	13
Western Europe	67	8	26	92	7	0	76	21	3	89	10	1
Central Europe	63	6	31	87	6	7	71	18	11	95	4	1
Africa	57	7	34	73	2	24	71	21	7	77	4	17
Middle East	33	3	65	34	0	65	93	6	1	92	0	8
Asia	48	9	43	78	3	18	64	32	4	79	6	16

Note: Limitations to market access and national treatment

Source: GATT secretariat

Table A3: Commitments on service activities by sub-sector (number of countries)

	Dvlpd	dvlpn	Transition	Total		dvlp	dvlpin	Transition	Total
1. Business					**6. Environment**				
A. Professional	22	13	3	39	A. Sewage	23	6	2	31
B. Computer	24	21	5	49	B. Refuse disposal	24	6	3	33
C. R & D	10	11	2	22	C. Sanitation	23	5	3	31
D. Real estate	23	3	0	25	D. Other	23	5	2	30
E. Rental/leasing	19	6	2	27	**7. Financial**				
F. Other	20	8	2	31	A. Insurance	25	37	5	67
2. Communication					B. Banking	23	21	3	48
A. Postal	0	3	0	3	C. Other	12	10	0	22
B. Courier	4	15	3	22	**8. Health**				
C. Telecom	11	12	3	26	A. Hospital	15	15	2	32
- Basic	1	8	0	9	B. Other human health	2	4	1	7
- Value Added	19	15	5	38	C. Social	13	1	1	15
D. Audio-visual	2	4	0	6	**9. Tourism and Travel**				
E. Other	6	0	6	12	A. Hotels and Restaurants	25	68	5	98
3. Construction					B. Travel agencies, tour operators	25	52	5	82
A. Buildings	24	21	4	49	C. Tourist guide	24	23	3	50
B. Civil engneering	24	20	4	48	D. Other	1	12	0	13
C. Installation and assembly	23	18	4	45	**10. Recreational, cultural, sporting**				
D. Completion and finishing	23	12	4	31	A. Entertainment	17	16	1	34
E. Other	20	13	3	36	B. News Agency	22	1	0	23
4. Distribution					C. Libraries, archives, museums	5	4	0	9
A. Commission agents	23	3	1	27	D. Sporting	20	15	1	36
B. Wholesale trade	25	7	5	37	E. Other	2	2	0	4
C. Retailing	25	8	5	38	**11. Transport**				
D. Franchising	23	5	3	31	A. Maritime transport	4	10	0	14
E. Other	14	0	0	14	B. Internal waterways	3	1	2	7
5. Education					C. Air	13	9	3	25
A. Primary	18	4	4	26	D. Space	2	0	0	2
B. Secondary	19	6	3	28	E. Rail	6	4	1	11
C. Higher	18	3	4	25	F. Road	17	6	1	24
D. Adult	18	1	4	23	G. Pipeline	2	1	1	4
E. Other	3	4	2	9	H. Auxiliary services	16	10	0	27
					I. Other	14	6	0	20

Note: Where sub-sectors are further disaggregated, figures refer to the average number of countries having made a commitment

Source: GATT secretariat

Bibliography

Adams, F. Gerard and Behrman, Jere (1982), *Commodity Exports and Economic Development.* Lexington, Mass.

Agosin, Manuel, Tussie, Diana and Crespi, Gustavo (1994), *Developing Countries and the Uruguay Round: An Evaluation and Issues for the Future*, Geneva: UNCTAD.

Anderson, Kym and Tyers, Rodney (1990), 'How Developing Countries Could Gain From Agricultural Trade Liberalization in the Uruguay Round', in Goldin, Ian and Knudsen, Odin (eds.), *Agricultural Trade Liberalization: Implications for Developing Countries*, Paris: OECD.

Askari, H. and Cummings, J.T. (1977), 'Estimating Agricultural Supply Response with the Nerlove Model', *International Economic Review,* 18(2).

Bond, Marian E. (1983), 'An Econometric Study of Primary Commodity Exports from the Developing Country Regions to the World', *IMD Staff Papers,* Washington DC: International Monetary Fund.

Chirathivat, Sutiphand (1992–3), Data supplied to author.

Chirathivat, S. (1991) 'Managing Thai Trade Policy to Better Access Developed Countries' Markets', *ASEAN Economic Bulletin.* 8(1).

Chavigny, Régis (1992), 'La Difficile Réorientation des Echanges des cinq pays d'Europe Central et Orientale', *Le Courrier des Pays de l'Est,* 373, October.

Collins, Susan and Rodrik, Dani (1991), *Eastern Europe and the Soviet Union in the World Economy,* Washington, D.C.: Institute for International Economics.

Davenport, Michael (1994), *Possible Improvements to the Generalized System of Preferences,* Geneva: report prepared for UNCTAD.

Davenport, Michael and Stevens, Christopher (1990), 'The Outlook for Tropical Products', in Stevens, Christopher and Doeke, C. Faber (eds.), *The Uruguay Round and Europe 1992, Implications for the Developing Countries,* Maastricht: European Centre for Development Policy Management .

Davenport, Michael (1988), *European Community Barriers to Tropical Agricultural Products,* Working Paper 27. London: Overseas Development Institute.

Department of Trade and Industry (1994), *The Uruguay Round of Multilateral Trade Negotiations 1986–94*, London: HMSO.

Duncan, R.C., (1990), *Policy Implications for Models,* in Goldin, Ian and Knudsen, Odin (eds.), *Agricultural Liberalisation: Implications for the Developing Countries*, Paris: OECD.

Erzan, Refiq, Goto, Junichi and Holmes, Paula (1990), 'Effects of the Multi-Fibre Arrangement on Developing Countries' Trade: An Empirical Investigation' in Carl B. Hamilton (ed.), *Textiles Trade and the Developing Countries*. Washington DC: World Bank.

Erzan, R. and Svedberg, P. (1989), *Protection Facing Exports from Sub-Saharan Africa in the EC, Japan, and the United States*, WPS 320, Washington DC: The World Bank, International Economics Department.

European Commission (1994), *Applying a Three-Year Scheme of Generalized Tariff Preferences (1995–97) in Respect of Certain Industrial Products Originating in Developing Countries*, 94/0209 (ACC) and *Extending into 1995 the Application of Regulations (EEC) No 3833/90, (EEC), No 3835/90 and (EEC) no 3900/91 Applying Generalized Tariff Preferences In Respect of Certain Agricultural Products Originating in Developing Countries*. Proposal for Council Regulation: Brussels: European Commission, 94/0210 (ACC) (referred to as EC, 1994 *GSP*).

European Commission (1994), *Integration of Developing Countries in the International Trading System: Role of the GSP 1995–2004*, Brussels: European Commission, June (referred to as EC, 1994 *Role of GSP*).

European Commission (1994), *The Uruguay Round: Global Agreement, Global Benefits*, Brussels: European Commission (referred to as EU, 1994 *Uruguay Round*).

Finger, J.M. and Olechowski, A. (1987), *The Uruguay Round: A Handbook on the Multilateral Trade Negotiations*, Washington DC: The World Bank.

GATT (1993), *An Analysis of the Proposed Uruguay Round Agreement, with Particular Emphasis on Aspects of Interest to Developing Economies*, Geneva: GATT. (referred to as GATT, 1994 *developing*).

GATT (1994), *General Agreement on Trade in Services: Country Offers* (All those available by 31 July 1994). Geneva: GATT.

GATT (1994), *Increases in Market Access Resulting from the Uruguay Round*, Geneva: GATT (referred to as GATT, 1994 *Access*).

GATT (1994), *Final Act Embodying the Results of the Uruguay Round of Multilateral Trade Negotiations*, Geneva: GATT (referred to as GATT, 1994 *Final Act*).

GATT (1993), *Overview of Developments in International Trade and the Trading System: Annual Report*, Geneva: GATT.

GATT (1986), *Text of the General Agreement*, Geneva: GATT.

GATT (1992), *Trade Policy Review – Bangladesh*. Vols I and II. Geneva (referred to as GATT, 1992 *Bangladesh*).

118

GATT (1993), *Trade Policy Review – Mexico*, Vols I and II. Geneva: GATT (referred to as GATT, 1993 *Mexico*).

Goldin, Ian, Knudsen, Odin and Van der Mensbrugghe, Dominique (1993), *Trade Liberalisation: Global Economic Implications*, Washington and Paris: World Bank and OECD

Grossman, Harald, Koopmaan, Georg and Michaelowa, Axel (1994), 'The New World Trade Organization: Pacemaker for World Trade?' *Intereconomics*, May/June.

Gould, David and Gruben, William C. (1994), *The Role of Intellectual Property Rights in Economic Growth*, Dallas: Federal Reserve Bank of Dallas, Working Paper 94-09.

Hamilton, C.B. and Winters, L.A. (1992), 'Opening up International Trade with Eastern Europe', *Economic Policy*, 14, April.

Hoekman, Bernard (1993), *Developing Countries and the Uruguay Round: Negotiations on Services*, Washington: World Bank, Policy Research Working Paper 1220.

Horlick, Gary N. (1993), 'How the GATT Became Protectionist – An Analysis of the Uruguay Round Draft Final Antidumping Code', *Journal of World Trade*, Vol 27, No. 5.

House of Commons (1994), *Hansard*, Volume 244, No. 133, Tuesday 14 June 1994. London: HMSO.

International Organisation of Consumers Unions (1994), *The Case for Openness: Consultation and Transparency in the World Trade Organisation*, London: IOCU.

IMF, *International Financial Statistics*, Monthly and Yearbooks. Washington DC: IMF.

Jackson, John H. (1994), 'Testimony to United States Senate Committee on Foreign Relations', *World Trade and Arbitration Materials*, vol. 6, No. 5. 215–36.

Japan Mission to the European Communities (1994), *News & Views from Japan*, Brussels: Mission of Japan.

Jonquières, Guy de (1994), 'Price of compromise', *Financial Times*, 25 November.

Kantor, M. (1993), Official Text of Briefing at National Press Club, December 20, 1993. London: United States Information Service.

Langhammer, Rolf J. (1992), *The Future of EC Trade Policy: Possible Effects for Latin America*. Madrid: IRELA.

Langhammer, Rolf J. (1983), *Problems affecting offers of the developing country tariff concessions round on south-south trade*. Working Paper 167. Keil: Keil Institute.

Luninck, Nicolaus (1993) 'GATT Dispute Settlement Mechanism Before and After Marrakesh 1994', London: report prepared for Overseas Development Institute.

Marville, R.O. (1994), *Will the Uruguay Round Result in an Important Loss of ACP Preferences on the European Union Market? If So, What Can Be Done By Way Of Compensation to ACP Countries?* London: CIIR.

McQueen, Matthew and Stevens, Christopher (1989), 'Trade Preferences and Lomé: Non-traditional ACP Exports to the EC', *Development Policy Review*, Vol 7, No. 3. London: Sage.

National Consumer Council (1994), *The Uruguay Round and Beyond: The Consumer View*, London: National Consumer Council.

Nguyen, Trien, Perroni, Carlo and Wigle, Randall (1993), 'An Evaluation of the Draft Final Act of the Uruguay Round', *Economic Journal*, November: Oxford and Cambridge, MA: Blackwell.

Organization of African Unity (1994), *Report of the Secretary-General on Preliminary Evaluation of the Results of the Uruguay Round of Multilateral Trade Negotiations of the General Agreement on Tariffs and Trade (GATT),* Addis Ababa: Organization of African Unity.

Page, Sheila, Davenport, Michael and Hewitt, Adrian (1991), *The GATT Uruguay Round: Effects on Developing Countries*, London: Overseas Development Institute.

Pescatore, Pierre (1993), 'The GATT Dispute Settlement Mechanism – Its Present Situation and its Prospects', *Journal of International Arbitration*, Geneva: 10.(1): 27–42

Schijndel, Anton van (1994), 'The Trouble with Bananas', *Financial Times,* 12 July, London.

Seade, Jesus (1994), *Africa and the Uruguay Round*, Geneva: GATT.

Sauvé, Pierre (1994), 'A First Look at Investment in the Final Act of the Uruguay Round', *Journal of World Trade*, 28: 5.

Silberston, Z.A. (1989), *The Future of the Multi-Fibre Arrangement.* London: HMSO.

Stern, Jon, Rhys, John, Rollo, Jim, Barraclough, Diana, Farrow, Elizabeth, Horton, Geoffrey and Rossert, Bertrand (1992), 'The Changes in Foreign Investment and Trade due to the Economic Reform in East and Central Europe and their Impact on the Regions of the Community in general and its Lagging Regions in particular', London: NERA for the CEC.

Sutherland, Peter D. (1994), *A New Framework for International Economic Relations*, Third Annual Hayek Memorial Lecture. Geneva: GATT, 30 June.

Sutherland, Peter D. (1994), *The World Trade Organization and the Future of the Multilateral Trading System.* Geneva: GATT, 30 May.

Sutherland, Peter D. (1994), *Global Trade – The Next Challenge*, World Economic Forum. Geneva: GATT, 28 January.

Sutherland, Peter D. (1994), 'Seeds of Doubt: Assurance on "Farmer's Privilege",' New Delhi: *Times of India*, 15 March 1994.

United Nations Statistical Office *Monthly Bulletin of Statistics*. New York: United Nations.

UNCTAD (1994), *The Outcome of the Uruguay Round: An Initial Assessment: Supporting Papers to the Trade and Development Report, 1994*, International Conference on the Uruguay Round of Multilateral Trade Negotiations, Tunis. New York: United Nations (referred to as UNCTAD, 1994 *Supplement*).

UNCTAD (1994), *Review of the Implementation, Maintenance, Improvement and Utilization of the Generalized System of Preferences*, Geneva: UNCTAD (referred to as UNCTAD, 1994 *GSP*)

UNCTAD (1993), *Handbook of International Trade and Development, 1992*, New York (referred to as UNCTAD, 1993 *Handbook*).

United Nations Development Programme (1994), *Services in Africa: Prospects for Trade, Regional Cooperation and Technical Assistance in the Post-Uruguay Round Period*

United Nations Economic Commission for Africa (1994), *Summary of the Impact of the Uruguay Round Agreements on Certain African Countries and the Technical Assistance Needs for their Implementation*. International Conference, Geneva, September.

UN Economic Commission for Asia (1994), *Identification of Critical Factors Likely to Influence Future Trade Outcomes in the Asian and Pacific Region and Recommendations on the Future Direction of Policy Oriented Work*, Conference Paper, September, Geneva: United Nations.

United States Department of Agriculture (1990), *Elasticities used in the USDA model on disk*, Washington

USITC (1991), *Annual Report on the Impact of the Caribbean Basin Economic Recovery Act on US Industry and Consumers*, 6th Report, 1990, USITC 2432, Washington: USITC.

Weston, Ann (1994), *The Uruguay Round: Unravelling the Implications for the Least Developed Countries and Low-Income Countries*, Geneva: UNCTAD.

Woodward, David (1994), *Reform of the EU Sugar Regime: Implications for Developing Countries' Sugar Exporters*, CIIR Occasional Paper, London: CIIR.

Yeats, Alexander (1994), *A Quantitative Assessment of the Uruguay Round's Effects and their Implications for Developing Countries*. Conference, Hebrew University.